A New Dress for Mona

A New Dress for Mona

A play by Mark Perry

DRAMA CIRCLE
Chapel Hill, North Carolina

Drama Circle
P.O. Box 3844
Chapel Hill, NC 27515 USA

Email: info@dramacircle.org
Website: www.dramacircle.org
www.anewdressformona.org

The play "A New Dress for Mona" is available for your group to produce. Visit the Drama Circle website for information on royalties and to apply for permission. No performance may be given without written permission.

Cover art by Jim Burns

ISBN: 978-0-9834701-3-7
Library of Congress Control Number: 2015908981

16 17 18 19 20 21 10 9 8 7 6 5 4 3 2 1

To the Bahá'ís of Iran

who continue to suffer
and continue to
point the way

On the day you put me in the grave

Remember my confusion

Remember all the fears I felt

Fill the little room

At the bottom of the tomb

With your light

I want to be part of your harvest of roses

I want to walk into your hall

Like an ant coming to see Solomon

All I want is your presence

And this silence

You finish this

Rumi

Table of Contents

ACT II

SUPPLEMENTARY MATERIALS

Acknowledgments

"A New Dress for Mona" is a major revision of the earlier play, "A Dress for Mona," which was published in 2002 by 5th Epoch Press. A multitude of people assisted in the development of that earlier work, many of whom were credited in that edition. Continued thanks go to Barry and Carol-lee Lane for their support of the piece including the production of a DVD of a 2003 performance. Also, mention must be made of Olya Roohizadegan's book *Olya's Story*, which was a primary source in the conception of the play.

For this recent edition, I relied heavily on the unpublished account written by Mona's mother, Mrs. Farkhundih Mahmudnizhad, and translated by Gloria Shahzadeh. Alexei Berteig helped craft a series of questions to Mrs. Mahmudnizhad in preparation for the proposed Jack Lenz film, "Mona's Dream." I must also thank Jack Lenz and David Hoffman, who encouraged me to explore the story cinematically, and Dara Marks, whose analysis of my writing was penetrating. My gratitude to Monir R. for her critical insights. Some readers I'd like to acknowledge: Martha, Maaman, Rahil, Kendall, Cindy and Ladan. Thanks also go to Mikko Kuitunen and Naantali Theatre (Finland) and also Hannah Mangenda and the University of KwaZulu-Natal cast for their helpful feedback. Acknowledgment must also go to those who have labored in translating the play: Migdalia Diez (Spanish), Mikko Kuitunen (Finnish), Peter Hoerster (German) and Mona Greenspoon (Thai). My gratitude goes out to McKay Coble, the UNC Department of Dramatic Art, and the director and cast of the 2010 UNC production—to Joseph Megel for his care and devotion to new work, to the cast that found the meaning of love in Mona's story, and to Lillian for her wholehearted embrace of Mona in the last days of her earthly life.

My loving gratitude goes to my wife, Azadeh, whose influence on and engagement with this play's development were enormous. I'd also like to acknowledge my parents for their support and encouragement over the years.

Introduction

On the 18th of June, 1983 in Shíráz, Iran, ten women were executed by hanging for their unwillingness to renounce their Bahá'í belief in the face of the Islamic fundamentalism that had recently overtaken their country. This act was particularly disturbing since usually only Bahá'í men were targeted for execution. The incident brought outcries from the world community appealing to the Iranian government to implement basic human rights for the Bahá'ís. This international pressure has had an effect in that recent years have thankfully witnessed no executions. Still, Bahá'ís are targeted by government smear campaigns and subject to arrest and long imprisonment for engaging in peaceful activities. They are denied basic rights of education, employment, assembly and legal protection. The Bahá'í Faith is a religion native to Iran and is considered apostasy by the religious leaders of Shí'ih Islam. Since the religion began in 1844, over 20,000 of its adherents have been martyred. Of the ten women executed that night in 1983, the youngest was 16 years old. Her name was Mona Mahmúdnizhád.*

Stories of saints are plentiful. Compelling and engaging plays about them are not. The lives of saints don't seem to be the stuff of which drama is made. Drama is about moral ambiguity, tragic flaws and comic vices. We want to see someone like us up on the stage, or better yet, someone worse off than us—someone who kills his father and sleeps with his mother! Oddly, we attain catharsis by watching some straw man, on whom we heap our repressed anxieties and desires, as he is beat about on stage by an ironic and moralizing Fate. (This may account as well for our laughter at comedy as our horror at tragedy.) On the other hand, the steady virtue of the saints, admirable though it may be, can hardly hold our attention, much less compete with the volatility of vice in dispensing pleasure. Perhaps we best leave the subject of sainthood to the stained-glass renderings of the Cathedral.

* There is some confusion among sources about Mona's age. Some say she was 16, some say 17, and some say 18. According to her sister, Taráneh, she was born 19 Shahrivar 1345 (10 September 1966 C.E.), which would make her 16 years 9 months and 8 days when she was executed. In the play, therefore, Mona is 16.

There they remain, in their two-dimensional splendor, floating up above us—stars in the sky—to be turned to in time of need, beseeched for a favor, for a guiding light.

Such a celestial entity to me was Mona. I remember as a young Bahá'í hearing the story, even in the national media, of the young exemplar of fortitude in the face of horrid abusiveness. In the mid-1980's, a Canadian musician named Doug Cameron released the song, "Mona with the Children," with an accompanying video that was effective in spreading the story. As songs generally do, it captured the emotion of the story, if less so the drama. And there was drama lurking there. The story felt like it could be told through theatre, except that Mona seemed super-human. How do we relate to someone like that?

I had the privilege in 1994 of hearing Olya Roohizadegan, one of Mona's fellow prisoners, speak. She had been released some months before the ten women were executed. One of the key points of her talk, and one that impressed me considerably, was the humanity of these people. Mona, this great figure, was really a *girl*—a girl of sixteen, who was remarkable in many ways, but who still had some of the same cares and concerns as so many others her age. She told the story of a dream Mona had before going into prison, a dream that would have a profound effect on her life. It was the dream of three dresses. Without going into the detail of the dream (since it provides a sort of backbone for the play), I can say that Mona's response in that dream was something I could understand, something I could relate to. I went home and wrote it down. I rarely do things like that.

Almost five years later, in contemplating what story I wanted to devote a summer to fashioning, I thought of Mona and her dream of three dresses. It was an "in," a place to begin. To me, her choice in the dream indicated a journey. It indicated Mona did not end where she began. By the time she was martyred, she had traversed vast spiritual territory. Now was it possible for us to benefit from her transformation in that special way theatre sometimes allows? I was willing to invest some time. The play eventually took a lot longer than a summer to come to fruition, but that was okay. The story has a power that has continued to sustain me, inspiring me to return to it.

In coming back to rewrite the play *A Dress for Mona*, my primary goal was to make it truer to the real story. This was made possible with the windfall of Mrs. Mahmudnizhad's remarkable, detailed notes. The result was almost a fully new play. *A New Dress for Mona* it would be therefore, and with more of Mona in it. The play is not though a document of history, and some liberty is taken with historical fact in service of—what is hoped to be—dramatic truth. The extensive notes that follow the play are meant to illuminate the real story and separate it out from the fictional elements of the play. These notes incidentally contain details of Mona's life never before published in English.

One tool in the hand of the playwright when approaching history is the conflation of time and place. One combines significant events that happened over a long time period and in many locales to concentrate sprawling Life into a series of easy-to-connect scenes. For example, there were 18 months between the execution scene that begins Act I and the arrest scene that ends it, but it seems to happen within a matter of days or weeks. Another tool when approaching history is the choice of factual or fictional characters. Here, Mona's family and the Bahá'í martyrs are all real, while all other characters are fictional, often being composites of the actual people involved in the events portrayed.

Perhaps the biggest departure the character Mona takes from the real Mona is in the underplaying of how extraordinary she was and the streamlining of the arc of her spiritual journey, in which her understandable desire for justice became an obstacle she had to transcend. This was a test for Mona, but when it peaked in her life who can say? Mona was precocious in the maturity of her faith and possessed astounding spiritual qualities well before going to prison. Then again tests in life come in waves and are not passed in one fell swoop as they are in plays. Clearly, to do what she did, Mona made that spiritual journey. And spiritual journeys imply going from weakness to strength, doubt to certainty, and fear to calm. Therefore Mona needs to be shown at times weak, doubting and fearful. The Rumi poem offered as an epigraph ("*remember my confusion... all the fears I felt*") is simultaneously an apology and a justification for this decision.

All this is of small consequence compared to the basic thrust of her service, suffering and sacrifice. That story, even in the briefest telling, can move the heart of the hearer. And Mona is just one bright star in one constellation in a vast sky brilliant with models of human attainment. The Bahá'ís of Iran have a secret to share. May their secret spread throughout the world, inspiring young and old everywhere to leave behind fear and hatred and to learn to see all with the eyes of love.

SETTING

Shiraz, Iran. 1982-83
(A few years into the Islamic Revolution)

CAST OF CHARACTERS

<table>
<tr><td>Mona (Mahmúdnizhád)</td><td>16; bright, passionate, single-minded, not yet a saint.</td></tr>
<tr><td>Father (Yadu'lláh Mahmúdnizhád)</td><td>50; gentle, loving, with a youthful exuberance and a compelling manner.</td></tr>
<tr><td>Mother (Fárkhundih Mahmúdnizhád)</td><td>40s; anxious, strong-willed, tender-hearted.</td></tr>
<tr><td>Árám</td><td>20ish. Quiet, with a poetic streak.</td></tr>
<tr><td>* Mulla</td><td>A powerful religious cleric, adamant.</td></tr>
<tr><td>* Farah</td><td>16; bold and worldly, Mona's friend.</td></tr>
<tr><td>* Mrs. Khudáyár</td><td>Middle-aged; loyal, a close neighbor.</td></tr>
<tr><td>* Taráneh (Mahmúdnizhád)</td><td>21; kind, pragmatic, Mona's sister.</td></tr>
<tr><td>* Guards 1 & 2</td><td>Members of the Revolutionary Guard.</td></tr>
<tr><td>* Woman in White</td><td>A messenger from the World of Light.</td></tr>
<tr><td>* Teacher (Female)</td><td>Narrow-minded, but not without pity.</td></tr>
<tr><td>* Rezá</td><td>20ish; a homebody, Mrs Khudayar's son.</td></tr>
<tr><td>* Shopkeeper (Male)</td><td>Opportunist who thinks he's principled.</td></tr>
<tr><td>* (Mr.) Ehsán (Mehdizadeh)</td><td>31. Bahá'í martyr and apparition.</td></tr>
</table>

** These roles may be assigned from among an* ENSEMBLE *of 6-8 actors, each of whom plays multiple characters. Other speaking and non-speaking roles include Mr. Vahdat, Mr. Khushkhú, students (female), worshipers, spirits, people on the street, vendors, young children, prisoners (female), guards, and baby Núrá.*

A NEW DRESS FOR MONA

A two-act play based on the life of
Mona Mahmúdnizhád (1966-1983)

ACT I

Scene 1 – Mona's home

A soft light illumines MONA, *alone.*

MONA: Iran, Iran—Once the pearl of the world, exalted among nations. You lit the Sacred Fire. You rebuilt the Holy Temple. Placed gifts before a newborn King. You took on the Prophet's mantle and embraced His family. Iran, my Iran—what has happened to you now? You raise up your enemies and mow down your friends. You lock up wisdom and lift the foolish. You reward thieves and sacrifice your heroes. How far you have fallen, Iran... and how ever will you rise again?

A night bird is heard. Lights come up. We see a large rug, a window frame, a tape recorder on a table, some candles and matches, plus a large poster board, paint, photos, scissors, and other crafts. MONA *is now on the rug and plays a recording of herself chanting. She lights three candles as she speaks the following names.*

MONA: Ehsán Mehdízádeh. Sattár Khushkhú. Yadu'lláh Vahdat.[1]

As she lights each candle, three blindfolded men are illuminated upstage one by one.

MONA: Friends, what can I offer up for you? I'd say my life, but I don't think God is interested in that. So I will paint you a picture.

She starts to paint. An execution scene starts to play out around her. The three men are in light, but the GUARDS *are not. They wear masks covering their mouths and noses.*

---

[1] See *Persian Pronunciation Guide* (p.129) for readings and pronunciations.

GUARD 1: Traitors! Heretics! You are to be executed now because of your crimes against Faith and Country. What do you have to say?

MR. KHUSHKHU: O God! Take me!

MR. VAHDAT: Guard! Come.

GUARD 1 *motions a younger guard,* ARAM, *towards* MR. VAHDAT.

GUARD 1: Go.

He goes.

MR. VAHDAT: You think I'm a traitor? My name is Vahdat. I was a colonel in the army.

GUARD 2: You were a colonel, then you became a... what was it?

GUARD 1: (*Taunting.*) Auxiliary Board Member!

GUARD 2: And for that you die! Plus the rest of you!

MR. KHUSHKHU: O God!

MR. VAHDAT: Take off my blindfold. I'll watch the bullets come.

ARAM *looks back to* GUARD 1, *who gestures him on. He removes the blindfold.*

MR. VAHDAT: (*Softly.*) Just don't aim for my heart. That does not belong to you.

MR. KHUSHKHU: O God!

GUARD 2: Be quiet!

EHSAN: Guard! Take mine off too. I will also welcome the bullets.

ARAM, *with clearance, goes to* EHSAN *and loosens his blindfold. The* GUARDS *are edgy, as if they're being mocked.*

GUARD 1: Okay!

ARAM *turns to go.*

EHSAN: Wait. Give me your hand.

EHSAN *kisses* ARAM*'s hand.* MONA*'s vision of the execution seems to pause and we see this detail disturbs her.*

ARAM & MONA: Why did you do that?

The execution resumes.

GUARD 2: No use begging for mercy! It's time to die!

GUARD 1: (*To a bewildered* ARAM.) Get back here, stupid!

ARAM *returns.*

GUARD 1: Ready!

MR. KHUSHKHU: We thought the days of the martyrs had ended.

GUARD 1: Aim!

GUARD 2: Aim for the heart!

The GUARDS *rain bullets on the men.* ARAM *is unable to raise his gun. Mona's* MOTHER *has entered.*

MOTHER: Mona?

MONA *has dipped a paintbrush into red paint and now brushes it liberally on the picture she is making.*

MOTHER: My God, girl, what are you doing?

MONA: Remembering the martyrs.

MOTHER: We don't know that it's true, Mona. That woman who brought the news, she's a very emotional type. They'll run you up and down the wall if you let them. Watch the rug. Look, your father has gone to find out what really happened. So until he comes, just put it outside your mind.

MONA *dips her hand in the red paint and begins to smear it over her picture.*

MOTHER: Now you're just trying to provoke me. Let's get your clothes ready for tomorrow. You haven't worn this green dress in a while, does it even fit now you're filling out?

No response.

MOTHER: What color are you going to wear?

MONA: Black.

MOTHER: (*Takes a deep breath.*) Don't you have homework?

MONA: I have an essay on how Islam brings freedom into our lives.

MOTHER: And?

MONA *looks at her as if the answer is self-evident.*

MOTHER: So talk to them about true Islam, not the regime, but the teachings of Muhammad: pray to God, give to the poor...

MONA: Why do you think Ehsan kissed the guard's hand?

MOTHER: We don't know that's true.

MONA: Who would make up such an odd detail?

MOTHER: Someone who wants attention! When people want attention, they embellish stories... (*Seeing the photos.*) You cut up all our pictures? Okay that's it. (*Blows out the candles.*) You need to just stop this and go to bed.

MONA: Mom, our friends have given their lives. What small sacrifice can we make?

She lights a match to relight the candles. The FATHER *is at the door.*

FATHER: Alláh-u-abhá. [2]

MONA: Dad. (*Blows out her match.*)

MOTHER: Tell us something good.

FATHER: (*After a beat.*) They're free.

MOTHER: What? What do you mean they're free? Free-free?

MONA: They're gone, Mom.

MOTHER: What? (*To* FATHER.) Then why didn't you say that? O God! I don't believe they killed them. (*Goes to leave.*) I don't know why you said that, Jamshid.

She is gone. MONA *has lain down on the carpet. The* FATHER *comes to her. They are quiet a while. He wipes her hand, caresses her hair.*

MONA: You're next, aren't you?

FATHER: We don't know that.

MONA: After Mr. Vahdat, you're next in line.

FATHER: Maybe things will calm down.

She hears the gunfire.

MONA: (*Without emotion, at first.*) So we're just supposed to lie down and let them roll right over us, mow us down one by one

[2] A Bahá'í greeting meaning 'God is most glorious.'

because we're a peaceful people they can scapegoat, we don't just not put up a fight, we welcome death, we welcome the bullets, we kiss their hands...

FATHER: Don't go too far now.

MONA: I'm not kissing anyone's hand.

She kisses his. He strokes her hair.

FATHER: Don't talk about this with your mother, okay?

MOTHER: (*Entering.*) What?

FATHER: (*Smiles gently.*) We have a funeral to arrange.

ACT I, Scene 2 – Mona's School

A school for girls. A STUDENT *fervidly reads aloud her essay.* MONA *is drawing a picture. Nearby is her friend,* FARAH.

STUDENT: Heaven opens its gates and calls out "Enter me!" Blood gathers on the ground and calls out "Avenge me!" The Revolution gathers momentum and calls out "Serve me!" Islam is the tree planted by Heaven watered by the blood of Revolution and its fruit calls out "Eat me!"

Some students giggle at this, including FARAH. *She turns to* MONA, *who is intent on her drawing.*

FARAH: (*Quietly.*) You're not drawing flowers today.

MONA *shakes her head.*

FARAH: Is that you?

MONA *nods her head.*

FARAH: You have fire in your eyes.

MONA: So watch out.

FARAH: What's going on?

MONA: (*Changing subject.*) Do you have your essay?

FARAH: Yeah. My brother wrote it.

MONA: I thought you were going to write this one yourself.

FARAH: I tried—swear to God, but the topic is so boring, so unrelated to my life. Just get me through this school year, and I'll live a hundred percent honest life. (*She smiles.*)

TEACHER: (*Unseen.*) Farah, would you like to read your essay?

FARAH *stands to read.*

FARAH: " 'The fruit of Islam is liberty and freedom of conscience, but you must taste it to understand.' Our great leader, Ayatu'llah Khomeini, has brought us back from the dangerous path of westernization the Shah was pursuing. We are returned now to the path of Muhammad, the Imams, and the law of the Qur'an. The West teaches that sweetness is found in boundless freedom, in material possessions, in satisfying the appetite, in alcohol, drugs, sex... (*She grimaces.*) Here they offer us a fruit that looks sweet, but tastes bitter, as they spread around the world this lie they call liberty when they only seek to enslave other nations in order to gain more themselves. But here is true sweetness, like a bite of ripe pomegranate: to submit to God's decree. May the righteous live forever with seventy-two virgins... And may the infidels burn until they turn black as coal." (*A beat.*) Sorry I got a little carried away at the end there.

TEACHER: Mona?

MONA *stands. She is timid at first, but soon grows impassioned.*

MONA: "Freedom. Of all the great words in this great wide world, freedom is the greatest. Throughout history, people have craved liberty. They've written about it, sung about it, fought for it, died for it. And yet, some men...

In the background, we see the silhouette of a religious cleric, MULLA, *ascending a pulpit.*

MONA: (*Cont'd.*) ... out of some perverse element of their soul that craves power and control, have insisted on denying liberty to others. They became like animals, like wolves in their pursuit, hunting down helpless gazelles, and they kill them, and roll in their blood, and their eyes roll back in their heads and so are blind to the evil they perpetrate...

TEACHER: I think that's enough.

MONA: (*Facing off.*) Why do you deny liberty to Bahá'ís?

Silence.

TEACHER: Sit down, Mona.

MONA: We are your countrymen, the same blood. Don't we have the right to live and believe what we will?

TEACHER: Stop right there.

MONA: What are you afraid of? That we'll steal away your freedom?

TEACHER: Students, turn your backs and put your fingers in your ears.

MONA: Or that we'll steal this veil you're hiding behind?!

TEACHER: Farah, you too! Right this minute.

The TEACHER *is now there, just outside of the lighted area.* FARAH *reluctantly turns her back on* MONA.

MONA: (*With fire in her eyes.*) Throw down that veil!

She throws down her paper. The STUDENT *who first read her essay traps it beneath her foot. Jump to next scene.*

ACT I, Scene 3 – A Mosque

The Islamic call to prayer is heard. The Shí'ih Muslim cleric, MULLA, *from the previous scene speaks, addressing a congregation.*

MULLA: The Revolution is triumphant! The light of Islam is spreading throughout the land! Praise be to God! He has sent our supreme leader, Ayatu'llah Khomeini, and has cast down the tyrant Shah. Many years we waited, many years while corruption festered, while he suppressed us and squandered the wealth of our nation on his passions and western friends. How does it feel now, Muhammad Reza? Now you are king over a few cubic meters of foreign dirt? (*Pause.*) Let us talk about a quiet corruption, let us talk about Bahá'í. Now Bahá'ís don't fight, and they don't force. They smile, and they help, and they trickle in like oil into your well water, like a potion in your tea. This corruption must be eradicated from this land. Where is the faithful believer who will assist me? For this is not only a revolution, but the Judgment, when the righteous and the sinners must be separated, and when those in the middle—who fail to take a side—will be hacked in two by the sword of God.

The crowd chants "Alláh-u-akbar" (God is great!) with exuberance. The MULLA *comes and joins* GUARD 1, *who attends as if protecting the* MULLA *as he walks through a crowd. The* MULLA *points out a woman.*

MULLA: See how beautiful this woman is? See how her beauty acts on you? How it starts bringing up your desire, driving your thoughts toward sexuality? This is the power of the devil. Not to say she's the devil, exactly, but her allure the devil uses to lead us astray. This is why we make hijab universally applicable. Now it's true most women don't get the fire going, but here in Shiraz, there are enough girls, a man can't walk in the street without seeing them with the short skirts and T-shirts. It's a good thing I have a robe like this, but a plain-clothes brother on the street...

GUARD 1: I think she wants to speak to you.

MULLA: (*Gestures him away.*) Flee the devil.

The GUARD *exits. The* MULLA *is approached by a* WOMAN *and her daughter (the* STUDENT *from the school scene). Both are shrouded in dark chadors and their voices cannot be heard.*

MULLA: Sister, I'm very happy you've come. This is your daughter, she must resemble more your husband. Of course, you can kiss my hand, but it's the Imam in me that accepts, otherwise those lips…

She kisses his hand.

MULLA: ... could give a horn to a holy man.

The daughter (STUDENT) *hands him Mona's paper.*

MULLA: What is this? (*Looks and listens.*) And the name of this Bahá'í girl? Hmm. I'll certainly look into that. You know, daughter, you should work in the company of men, your appearance is highly conducive to an atmosphere of chastity.

Another kiss for the hand.

MULLA: Another kiss then? Oh, and the daughter. Well, okay.

The two are gone. GUARD 1 *returns with* ARAM, *the reluctant guard from Scene 1.*

MULLA: These Shirazi women!

GUARD 1: Your eminence, you remember my cousin, Aram?

MULLA: He looks like he needs some sleep. What's going on with these Bahá'ís? What happened at the cemetery today?

GUARD 1: (*Caught off guard.*) Nothing, things were fine, we were in control. (*A beat.*) People get emotional sometimes.

MULLA: (*Unsatisfied, to* ARAM.) Were you there?

ARAM: Yes, sir.

EHSAN, *the martyr from Scene 1, has entered, now as an apparition. He stares at* ARAM.

MULLA: And?

ARAM: I was just trying to keep calm.

MULLA: So they were making trouble?

GUARD 1: We had it under control.

MULLA: Not you. (*To* ARAM.) They were angry?

ARAM: They were mourning. Some were angry.

MULLA: The Bahá'ís?

EHSAN *has opened his coat to reveal blood.*

ARAM: I couldn't tell Bahá'ís from Muslims.

MULLA: You can always tell. (*Points to his own eyes.*) Would you like me to teach you how?

ARAM: I like to learn.

MULLA: Oh, he's slippery. That wasn't what I asked you.

GUARD 1: He's a poet-type, sir.

MULLA: A poet? So, Hafez, let's hear one.

ARAM: My memory's not so good.

MULLA: So compose one. I'll give you a subject: the Bahá'ís. Who was it you were following?

EHSAN *has come close to* ARAM.

ARAM: Ehsan.

MULLA: Last name, I mean.

ARAM: Mehdizadeh.

MULLA: Good memory. So describe him—no poem necessary, just a word.

EHSAN *takes* ARAM*'s hand to kiss.*

GUARD 1: Say something, Aram. He was a spy, a traitor.

MULLA: (*To* GUARD 1.) Shut up. (*To* ARAM.) Hafez?

ARAM: (*After a pause.*) Mystifying.

GUARD 1: (*Hits* ARAM *on the head.*) Idiot!

MULLA: Shut up! Go bring me my rug. It's time for prayer.

The GUARD *goes to kiss the* MULLA*'s hand, but he's waved away.*

MULLA: You live in your thoughts, don't you, young man? Yes, some of the Bahá'ís seem to embody remarkable virtue, whether forgiveness, courage... tolerance for pain. But true virtue is born of submission to God's will, you see?

ARAM *gestures as if he has heard and is considering the matter. He watches* EHSAN *move away.*

MULLA: Okay, Hafez, I'll be looking for a job for you, one we wouldn't want to waste on just any lughead.

GUARD 1 *is back with the prayer rug. The* MULLA *offers his hand in dismissal to* ARAM, *who goes to shake it. The* MULLA *is surprised, but not phased. When* ARAM *goes to pull away his hand, the* MULLA *holds it, twists it just so, looks it over.*

MULLA: Soft. What would people say if they saw that the Revolutionary Guard had such soft hands?

The call to prayer has begun again. The MULLA *goes into his preparations. The* GUARD *gives* ARAM *a look.*

ACT I, Scene 4 – Mona's Home

MONA *and her* MOTHER *enter—the* MOTHER *with a dark chador, which she removes and folds up upon entering.*

MOTHER: Your father already has so much on his mind with the martyrs needing burial and the guards refusing us going in to the cemetery... It's only because he pleaded with that man that you weren't expelled.

MONA: You should have let them do it.

MOTHER: Are you so ungrateful? You're one of the few Bahá'í children still in school.

MONA: What am I learning? Propaganda! It's not like I can go to university anyway.

MOTHER: Look, we are going to get through this. These mullas can't stay in power long. The people will see the violence and they'll say enough is enough.

MONA: We can't just wait to be rescued while they sweep into our homes and take what we love.

MOTHER: They won't. God won't let them.

MONA: God let them into Mr. Vahdat's home. Being a Bahá'í is no protection—that goes for Dad too.

MOTHER: Your father is going to be fine! People were mad they couldn't go pay their respects to the dead. The Muslims, I mean. They will push back...

MONA: In one hundred forty years, when have the people of this country ever stood up for us? (*A beat.*) We have to sound the alarm, remind them that this is Iran, the land of Cyrus the Great, the founder of human rights! That's what I was standing up for today.

MOTHER: Did it work?

MONA: Did what work?

MOTHER: Your wake up call.

MONA: No, because the teacher made them put their fingers in their ears.

MOTHER: And this is what they will continue to do if we speak to them harshly.

MONA: What does God want us to do, Mom? If He just shows me the path, I'll go. I just don't understand why there has to be so much pain. (*Waits for an answer.*)

MOTHER: Why are you looking at me?

A knock. The door opens. It's Mona's sister, TARANEH, *21 and pregnant.*

MOTHER: Taraneh!

TARANEH: Hey, I got here as soon as I could.

MOTHER: You need to talk some sense into this sister of yours.

MONA: Ah, ah, ah, ah, ah....

MONA *goes right for* TARANEH*'s belly. She kneels and touches.*

TARANEH: Hi darling.

MONA: (*Absorbed.*) I can't believe this is you, Taraneh. There's a little creation forming inside of you.

TARANEH: Yeah, I'm inflating like a balloon. God, I hope I can save my skin.

MONA: (*In her own world, but not leaving* TARANEH*'s belly.*) But imagine what the baby is going through, no idea where life is leading. Bahá'u'lláh says we're like the baby in the womb and the spiritual world is all around us. You know, like we're inside, hidden by this veil... (*Indicates her belly.*) All warm, we'd stay inside there forever.

TARANEH: All your meals delivered, I can't believe what food this kid orders, things I never would eat, but she wants it, she gets it.

MOTHER: She?

TARANEH: Did I say that? I keep telling myself not to. (*Tears well up.*) I don't even want a girl. I think Sírús's family wants a boy—they won't say it, but they keep calling it a "he."

MOTHER: We need a boy in the family.

MONA *has her ear up to* TARANEH*'s belly.*

TARANEH: What do you think, sweetie?

MONA: I'm listening. (*Addresses the baby.*) Who are you? Helloooo.... Hellooooo.....

A shift where focus comes in on MONA *and* TARANEH*'s belly and off the* MOTHER *and* TARANEH*'s actions.* MONA *sees a beautiful* WOMAN IN WHITE.

MONA: Who are you?

The ceiling seems to open and light starts coming down—a glimmering of the possible.

WOMAN IN WHITE: (*With gentle authority.*) Prepare yourself. Just like the expectant mother, just like the babe—prepare yourself.

MONA: For what?

The WOMAN *shrugs as if to say "what else?"*

MOTHER: Mona?

Shift back to the physical plane.

TARANEH: Ouch. Honey, you're squeezing a little tight there.

MONA: (*Coming back to herself.*) Huh?

TARANEH: What's wrong? You see a ghost?

MONA: (*Standing.*) No, I'm fine.

MONA *exits.*

MOTHER: What am I going to do with this girl? She's in her own world half the time, and who can blame her? This one is such a mess, but I'm really starting to worry. What if they come for your father? She's so attached to him. I catch them sometimes just staring at each other as if they're reading each other's minds. I think they don't want me to know how they're feeling, like it will crush me. It won't! (*She sits.*) I don't know that we shouldn't get out of Iran altogether at least until this whole thing blows over.

TARANEH: Have you talked to Dad?

MOTHER: When do I see him? Anyway, he won't talk about it.

TARANEH: Where is he now?

MOTHER: Where is he ever? Out feeding the poor, healing the sick...

TARANEH: Mom.

MOTHER: I'm sorry, but what about us? And now I see Mona going the same way—you know she's going to this orphanage three times a week now, these tiny neglected kids call her "Mommy Mona," and she just melts. Then she comes home, and the smell! I mean, that's fine, it's great, but the girl doesn't communicate with me! We never had that trouble, you and me, did we?

MRS. KHUDAYAR, *a neighbor, enters.*

MRS. KHUDAYAR: Well, are you coming?

TARANEH: Hello, Mrs. Khudayar.

MOTHER: Coming where?

TARANEH: The birthday party, Mom. I'll get Mona. (*Exits.*)

MOTHER: I can't believe I forgot. What time? Wait til you hear...

MRS. KHUDAYAR: He's just about to cut the cake.

The voice of her son, REZA, *is heard from the hall.*

REZA: (*Off.*) Is she coming?

TARANEH: (*Having reentered.*) Maybe a little later.

REZA: (*Poking his head in.*) Why not now?

TARANEH: Happy birthday, Reza.

MOTHER: Mona has some thinking to do.

MRS. KHUDAYAR: Thinking, huh?

REZA: (*Exiting.*) Fine.

MRS. KHUDAYAR: I keep telling him to get it out of his head, but listen to me? God help us, these little boys grow to be men.

TARANEH: Well, shall we get some cake?

MRS. KHUDAYAR: Well, well, Taraneh, look at you. Wait, wait.

She feels her hair, hikes up her skirt to look at her ankles and legs, feels around her stomach and chest, etc. Then when the exam is over.

MRS. KHUDAYAR: Definitely a girl!

They exit. MONA *reenters, checks the door and peeks around where the* WOMAN IN WHITE *appeared. Finding nothing, she makes a decision and starts to set up her art supplies in a way reminiscent of the first scene. She plays her tape recorder, lights a candle and begins to paint.*

ACT I, Scene 5 – Mona's Dream

MONA *is stretched out asleep. The* WOMAN IN WHITE *from the previous scene enters, radiant. A number of figures,* SPIRITS, *enter.* ARAM *is upstage center, a white shroud thrown over him. The* WOMAN IN WHITE *wakes* MONA *and brings her to her feet.*

WOMAN IN WHITE: I have something for you. A gift. But you must choose.

As MONA *orients herself, three* SPIRITS *with gift boxes come forward. The* WOMAN IN WHITE *gestures* MONA *to the first.* MONA *opens the box and pulls out a beautiful red dress.*

MONA: Ooh.

SPIRIT 1: Red. The final testimony, indisputable truth; blood spilled presents its own proof. Red is a fire, a lover, a warning. The sun descending has no finer adorning.

MONA *holds the dress up to herself. There is an instant scene shift to a girl being executed by hanging.* MONA *shudders and pushes the dress away.*

MONA: No!

In an instant, the scene shifts back and that dress is whisked away. The WOMAN IN WHITE *gestures* MONA *towards the second box.* MONA *goes and pulls out a black dress of the same pattern.*

MONA: Lovely.

SPIRIT 2: Black. Wrapping itself about, the jealous lover douses all other color. Pupil of the eye, closed lid of night; black is nothing without light.

She holds this dress up to herself. An instant scene shift where several people are suffering intolerably, from torture or deprivation. MONA *pushes this one away as well.*

MONA: No, I don't want that one either.

The scene shifts back, but MONA *is hesitant to open the third box. The* WOMAN IN WHITE *smiles and opens it for her. She pulls out a blue dress.*

MONA: I like blue. (*She takes it, but hesitates to put it up to herself.*) But what is it?

SPIRIT 3: Blue is the beginning, sea and sky, renewal. A soul alone, a stone, a pool. Ripples and reflections that sparkle over faces, good deeds that light up darkened places.

Here the WOMAN IN WHITE *comes close and whispers in her ear.* MONA *hears, holds the dress up to herself.*

WOMAN IN WHITE: Do you want to remove the veil?

MONA *looks at her with all sincerity and nods. The* WOMAN IN WHITE *nods as well. All attention shifts to the shrouded* ARAM. MONA *walks up to him and with a breath pulls off the veil. An unworldly power and radiance rolls off him, and* MONA *is awestruck. All others look away out of reverence.* MONA *has dropped to her knees and stares.*

WOMAN IN WHITE: Enough!

The dream is over. Lighting shift. All leave except ARAM *and* MONA, *who tosses in sleep on the rug and cries out as if falling. Her* FATHER *is there at the door.*

FATHER: Honey? (*He goes to her.*) Wake up, sweetheart.

MONA: (*Waking, crying out.*) Ah! Ah! Dad, Dad...

FATHER: It's okay, sweetie. It's just a dream.

MONA: Dad, I saw Him. I saw Him.

FATHER: It's okay...

MONA: I saw His face.

ARAM *has remained in the same place, as if he's still in Mona's sight.*

ACT I, Scene 6 – A Clothing Shop off a busy street

A SHOPKEEPER *fiddles with a tape recorder that plays music by Dariush, a popular Iranian singer. He sings aloud to a sad, albeit Western-influenced song.* MONA *enters energetically, interrupting him.*

MONA: Salaam.

SHOPKEEPER: (*Wary, turning down the music.*) Salaam.

MONA *is on a mission, searching through the clothes.* FARAH *enters.*

FARAH: Mona, why didn't you wait up for me?

SHOPKEEPER: Salaam.

FARAH: Hi. (*To* MONA.) Are you still mad about the class?

No response.

FARAH: I'm sorry, but what was I supposed to do? Everyone was freaking out, looking at me with all this hate, and the teacher singled me out...!

SHOPKEEPER: Girls, we just got in some nice scarves...

MONA: No thank you.

FARAH: Look, if anyone should be mad, it should be me. You're the one who made a scene, and they all know I'm your friend.

MONA *looks at her.*

FARAH: Got you to look.

MONA *looks away.*

FARAH: Come on, don't be mad at me.

MONA: I'm not mad. If no one will stand up for us, even our friends, when things get tough, that's fine.

FARAH: I told you I was sorry.

MONA: So I forgive you.

FARAH: But you're still mad. You can't forgive someone and still be mad at them.

MONA: I don't want to talk about it. If you want, you can help me look for a dress.

FARAH: Okay. (*A beat.*) How about a red one?

MONA *looks at her, a little spooked.*

FARAH: Red for anger.

SHOPKEEPER: Very good prices on these scarves, the best in the city!

FARAH: No thanks!

MONA: I don't want red. I want blue. I had a dream last night and I was offered a choice of red, black or blue dresses, and so I chose blue.

FARAH: Offered by who?

MONA: By God. I think.

FARAH: Wow. Why do you think God wants you to have a blue dress?

MONA: The dresses symbolized paths I could choose in my life.

FARAH: Okay.

MONA: The red one meant martyrdom and the black one suffering.

FARAH: Someone would choose those paths?

MONA: I chose the last one, which was service.

FARAH: So…

MONA: I chose a life of service.

FARAH: What about a life of fun?

SHOPKEEPER: (*Approaching.*) How can I help you girls?

MONA: Do you have any dresses this color?

SHOPKEEPER: Sure. Over there.

MONA *moves to the indicated area. The* SHOPKEEPER *sees* ARAM *standing just outside the shop door looking in, and he goes to switch cassette tapes.*

SHOPKEEPER: How did that tape get in there? That music's unclean! (*Switches tapes to something more Islamic.*) Much better.

ARAM *seems to take no notice, but stares at* MONA. *He wears nothing that might distinguish him as a guard.*

FARAH: So maybe you're going to get married.

MONA: What?

FARAH: How else do women serve in Iran? They keep the rice cooking and the babies coming.

SHOPKEEPER: (*Back to help.*) God willing. How about this one?

MONA: Mmm, that one.

She chooses a blue closer to the dream color and turns to the mirror. FARAH *browses, then approaches her.*

FARAH: So was there a guy in this dream?

MONA, *having seen* ARAM, *stands transfixed, and points to him. He sees her point and looks away.*

FARAH: What, him?

MONA: (*Folding up.*) Maybe we should buy this and go.

ARAM *is still in sight.* MONA *glances at him as she goes to pay.*

MONA: How much?

SHOPKEEPER: For you: 100.

FARAH: Rial?

SHOPKEEPER: (*Sarcastic.*) Rial. 100 Tuman.

MONA: Sorry I don't have that much.

SHOPKEEPER: Why don't you ask your boyfriend? (*Indicates* ARAM.)

MONA: He's not my boyfriend.

FARAH: Who made you a mulla to judge?

SHOPKEEPER: I have a reputation to keep. Girls like you come in with no scarves, flirting with boys, acting like this is the time of the Shah? Now if you covered your hair like chaste Muslim girls…

MONA: (*Calmly.*) Well, I'm not a chaste Muslim, I'm a chaste Bahá'í. And I can offer you 20 tuman.

FARAH: (*Flummoxed.*) You don't need to tell him that.

SHOPKEEPER: Bábí?

MONA: Bahá'í. They stopped calling us Bábís a hundred years ago.

SHOPKEEPER: Bábí báhí, I don't care. (*He takes the dress back.*) 200 tuman! Final price.

MONA: Sir, be fair. All religions teach that much. (*She pulls out money.*) Now how much is the dress worth? I have twenty-five tuman.

A beat. He looks at her money.

SHOPKEEPER: Out.

MONA: What?

SHOPKEEPER: The dress is not for sale, Bábí girl!

MONA: It's Bahá'í. Bahá'í, Bahá'í, Bahá'í, Bahá'í!

FARAH *walks away.*

MONA: What is the big deal that no one can stand to hear that word?

SHOPKEEPER: Get out!

MONA: Fine. See you, Farah.

On her way out, she passes by ARAM. *They have a moment, and she turns and leaves.*

FARAH: Wait up, Mona! (*To* ARAM.) What are you staring at?

She leaves. ARAM *pulls a photograph from a small notebook, looks at it, then towards where* MONA *exited.* EHSAN *is now there, but* ARAM *avoids looking at him.*

SHOPKEEPER: You go now, you'll lose your girlfriends.

EHSAN *is gone.* ARAM *turns and walks into the shop and picks up the cassette tape of Dariush the* SHOPKEEPER *was playing. He shakes it and puts it up to his ear as if to listen to it. He then raises his eyebrows at the* SHOPKEEPER, *who freezes.*

ACT I, Scene 7 – Mona's Home

Mona's FATHER *and* MOTHER *sit quietly in their living room. There is tension in the air, as if he's delivered news she did not want to hear.*

FATHER: Aren't you going to say something?

MOTHER: What do you want me to say? You're not coming to me asking me my opinion on this.

He is silent.

MOTHER: Have you thought about the impact this will have on Mona?

FATHER: Yes.

MOTHER: She needs a father.

FATHER: Farkhundih.

MOTHER: I am not blowing this out of proportion—

MONA *enters through the front door, mumbling under her breath. She slips off her shoes.*

MONA: Alláh-u-abhá. (*She heads towards her room.*)

MOTHER: Mona, come back here, please.

MONA: (*Returning.*) What's going on?

MOTHER: You told me you'd be back before this. This place needs to be cleaned. I'm going shopping. I'm writing a list for you. I want you to get started right away—

MONA: Okay.

MOTHER: I'm not happy about you being gone when there's so much to do. (*She exits to the bedroom.*)

MONA: What happened?

FATHER: It's okay. (*Exits to kitchen.*) You want a little tea?

MONA: (*Sits on the carpet and holds her head.*) I don't know. (*A beat.*) I saw God today... on the street.

FATHER: (*Reentering.*) You did.

The FATHER *has put the kettle on and now somewhat distractedly tries to straighten up the apartment, which in truth is already quite tidy.*

MONA: There's this path opening in front of me, but it's totally dark. I can't seem to open my eyes wide enough to take it in.

MOTHER: (*Entering, moving to the door.*) Here's the list, Mona, so don't forget. (*At the door.*) There's a package here. Maybe it's a bomb.

She kicks it inside the door and leaves. The FATHER *winces some and holds his stomach.*

FATHER: Mmm.

MONA: Your tummy? Here, let me do that (*She takes the broom.*)

FATHER: I'm okay, I'll just get the tea. (*Exits.*)

MONA: (*Starting, then stopping the sweeping.*) Here's what I figure. I'm not supposed to have that dress. It's just a symbol. I mean, obviously, He told me it stands for service. So I don't need the actual dress for that. It's better that I don't have it.

FATHER: (*Off.*) Uh-huh.

MONA: The young man is a symbol too. He's... the "man on the street"—meaning, I'm supposed to serve everyone, no matter where I am. And... I don't have to go looking for it like I did with the dress. Service will find me. What do you think?

FATHER: Sorry, honey, the kettle was making noise.

He has entered with a tray with tea. He has been crying and turns to wipe away tears.

MONA: Are you sure everything's all right?

There's a knock at the door. We hear the neighbor, MRS KHUDAYAR.

MRS. KHUDAYAR: (*Off.*) Hello!

MONA: (*At the door.*) It's our neighbor.

FATHER: (*Uncertain what to do with the tea tray.*) I better not.

He exits back into the kitchen.

MONA: Dad, come back.

FATHER: (*Off.*) Mona, we can't push people.

MONA: (*Shakes her head and opens the door.*) Hello, Mrs. Khudayar.

MRS. KHUDAYAR: Am I interrupting?

MONA: No, Dad was just making some tea.

MRS. KHUDAYAR: (*So the* FATHER *can hear—*) No thank you.

FATHER: (*Off.*) Hello, Mrs. Khudayar.

MRS. KHUDAYAR: So, Mona, your mother was telling me about your dream—three dresses, that's wonderful!

MONA: Well, it wasn't about dresses really...

MRS. KHUDAYAR: Oh?

MONA: It was really about choices in life...

MRS. KHUDAYAR: Mona, if you just say yes to this boy, these dreams won't haunt you any more.

MONA: What?

MRS. KHUDAYAR: Oh, as if...! Oh! (*Aside to* MONA.) Your father doesn't know yet? The boy who's following you. It's been days now I've seen him.

MONA: What does he look like?

MRS. KHUDAYAR: See for yourself. You can probably spot him out that window.

MONA *walks over and looks out the window, sees him and responds by pulling away and then looking again.*

MRS. KHUDAYAR: (*Excited.*) Oh, oh, oh—do you know him?

MONA: (*Almost to herself.*) That's the same young man as was in my dream.

MRS. KHUDAYAR: Oh, that's so precious. Run away with him! I mean, with your parents' permission and all—

MONA: That wasn't really the spirit of the dream. He was just…

MRS. KHUDAYAR: Just what?

MONA: A symbol.

MRS. KHUDAYAR: Symbol! I don't know about you girls today, with so many boys swarming around you, you take it for granted, then you become my age and you're invisible and have to get your pleasure by watching others, but you're giving me absolutely no pleasure!

MONA: Dad, isn't that tea ready yet?

MRS. KHUDAYAR: Girl, how old are you?

MONA: Sixteen.

MRS. KHUDAYAR: When I was sixteen, I was already married with a loaf in the oven. You're not going to get any more beautiful, my dear.

The FATHER *enters with the tea, still fighting off his stomach pain.*

FATHER: Here we are…

MRS. KHUDAYAR: Look at the time, and I just dropped by to give you some mail, which they delivered to the wrong address. There's one for you, Mona. It arrived unsealed—those goons with the Revolutionary Guard can't admit they're censoring the mail so they try to put it off on me.

MONA: (*Taking the envelope.*) Wait, won't you have some tea with us?

MRS. KHUDAYAR: (*Going.*) That son of mine is going to be home any moment. He was so disappointed you missed his party—Such a lovely rug!

MONA: Mrs. Khudayar, why don't you ever have tea with us?

FATHER: Mona, if she needs to go…

MRS. KHUDAYAR: I have tea at home.

MONA: I know, but we always offer and you never accept.

FATHER: Mona dear.

MRS. KHUDAYAR: No, it's okay. The truth is that from the time I was a little girl, I have been told that your tea—Bahá'í tea—is a potion that brainwashes people to become Bahá'ís.

MONA: But that's silly.

MRS. KHUDAYAR: I know, but what can I do? I guess I'm brainwashed myself. (*Leaving.*) Looks like a package here. Maybe it's from an admirer. (*She winks and leaves.*)

MONA: Don't say anything, Dad. We have to confront these people... as a service to them.

FATHER: (*Unconvinced.*) What's the letter?

MONA: It's been opened.

FATHER: Who's it from?

MONA: (*Opens the letter and reads.*) It's from the Bahá'í children's committee.

FATHER: Yeah?

MONA: They want me to teach a Bahá'í children's class.

FATHER: Let me see.

MONA: (*Moved.*) It's happening, Dad. I asked Him to show me the path and He's doing it.

FATHER: (*Taking the letter.*) I'm just surprised the committee didn't hand-deliver it.

MONA: (*Goes for the package by the door.*) Could be from an admirer. Could be a bomb. (*Picks it up.*) Why was Mom so upset? Before I die.

FATHER: I've been appointed to the Auxiliary Board.

MONA: (*After a beat.*) That's such an honor.

FATHER: And she's worried, obviously, about the exposure.

MONA: (*Covering her emotion.*) Just leave me your books—Taraneh wants them too, but I'll use them more.

FATHER: Mona, I know it's scary, but you know this path God is laying out before you? I have mine too. And your mother has hers. And if God decides that our paths should diverge, I need you to be strong. Okay?

He kisses her and turns to go. She opens the package and pulls out the blue dress from the shop.

MONA: Dad.

He turns.

MONA: Farah must have gone back... (*Holds it up to herself.*)

FATHER: It's as if Bahá'u'lláh picked it out Himself.

Shift of scene. MONA *comes forward as if to a mirror with the dress.*

MONA: It's a new dress for Mona. And a new Mona must step into it.

ACT I, Scene 8 – A Street in Shiraz

People are coming and going: men freely, women less so. Birds and traffic are heard. ARAM *waits, apparently for* MONA. *He is preoccupied, apparently writing a poem in his notebook. He recites some lines aloud to test them out.*

ARAM: In a perfect world... In a perfect world, there would be no... No... (*Searching for the word.*) Division? Distance? No you and me, but only we. (*Smiles at this, scribbles and continues reading a line he already has.*) But now I follow, I follow, I follow behind.

He then looks up to see EHSAN *before him. He looks away, moved, as if the brief moments of respite only refresh the agony. The* MULLA *enters with* GUARD 2. *The* MULLA *has an unopened pomegranate.*

MULLA: Hafez! I've been wondering about you.

ARAM: Hello, sir.

MULLA: So? (*Hands* GUARD 2 *the pomegranate.*) Open that up.

GUARD 2 *looks at him quizzically. The* MULLA *focuses in on* ARAM, *waits.*

ARAM: (*Shrugs.*) Just a sweet girl.

MULLA: So she isn't speaking out at all about her religion?

ARAM: Really just going to school, visiting the orphanage... She went shopping with a friend.

MULLA: For what?

ARAM: A dress. I think. Maybe a scarf...

MULLA: (*After a beat.*) Okay. (*To* GUARD 2, *who is vigorously going at the pomegranate.*) Easy there. (*He grabs some seeds and puts them in his mouth. To* ARAM.) Let me see her picture again?

ARAM: Oh. (*Takes the picture out of his notebook.*) I'd be happy to keep it, I mean keep an eye on her.

MULLA: (*Looks at the picture, smiles.*) I'm sure you would. (*Takes back the pomegranate from* GUARD 2, *puts more seeds in his mouth. To* ARAM.) Keep a log of everything she does. It'll help us make a case against the father.

He exits with GUARD 2. ARAM *returns to writing in his little notebook, just as* MONA *and* TARANEH *enter.* TARANEH *wears a loose headscarf and waddles as she walks.* MONA, *wearing the blue dress, walks with a spring in her step and carries a bag with materials and snacks for her children's class.*

TARANEH: (*Offhandedly.*) I don't know, you know, she's Mom, and Mom's not Dad. They're not in the same place. None of us are. I don't even know where I am, and carrying this life inside me, literally creating it as we speak, and I don't know the first thing about her, or him... whatever. So you have your lesson for the kids?

MONA: Yes. (*Sees* ARAM *waiting for her.*) Hello.

She and TARANEH *walk past.* TARANEH *adjusts her scarf.*

TARANEH: You know him?

MONA *doesn't answer as they exit.* ARAM *smiles wistfully, finishes a thought he was writing in his little notebook, and then walks off after* MONA.

ACT I, Scene 9 – The Children's Class

MONA *tells a story to a group of children about 6 or 7 years of age. She is animated, gentle and luminous when she is with the children*

MONA: Once upon a time, there was a lover named Majnun and his love was the beautiful princess, Layli. Majnun was a good man, a pure man, and he had no thought but for his Layli. The problem was he had been separated from her for such a long time that he got very, very sad. One night, he was so sad, he went out into the city hoping to die. And he walked and walked the streets, crying, until a watchman saw him. This was one of the guards in the city. So the watchman started to follow him, and Majnun got scared. He thought the watchman was coming to hurt him. So he walked faster. And the watchman walked faster. And Majnun started to run. And the watchman started to run, and then another watchman came after him, and then another. Certainly these men would kill him, he thought. And so Majnun ran and ran until he got trapped with a tall wall in front of him and all the watchmen behind him. So what do you think he did? He ran to the wall, the men came after him, and so he jumped and he climbed, and the wall was very high, and he worked so hard and they could almost reach him, but with his last bit of strength, he threw himself over the wall not knowing what was on the other side. And he fell and he fell and he landed, plop. And it was soft and green. He was in a beautiful garden, and when he looked, who did he see but Layli walking in the garden, a lamp in her hand, searching for a ring she had lost. So what do you think Majnun did? He cried out in joy, and he thanked God and he thanked the watchmen who had led him to his heart's desire, and he understood that these men he thought were mean and bad and scary actually had done him the greatest service. And he wondered, why couldn't I see that before?

As she has been finishing this story, ARAM *has appeared in the background, looking in, as if through a window, then he walks off.*

MONA: Did you like that story? That's a story Bahá'u'lláh told. Yes, sweetie.

A child has a question.

MONA: Well, it means that God asks us to be patient with the difficult things in our lives, because what we love most God will never ever really take away even though it may feel like it. What do you love most? Your Mommy and Daddy? (*Smitten and moved.*) Me too. So who wants some cheese puffs?

ACT I, Scene 10 – The Street Outside

FARAH *waits outside where* MONA *has been teaching.* MONA *comes in, high as a kite from being around the children.*

MONA: Farah! I didn't expect you here.

FARAH: I was hoping I could catch you.

MONA: Did you see all my kids?? Aren't they adorable? I just love them so much. I tell you, I feel like I'm right there with God when I'm with them, they fill me with so much light.

FARAH: Yeah, they're cute—you're not mad at me.

MONA: How could I be mad?

FARAH: Cause of the shop.

MONA: (*She models her dress.*) Look!

FARAH: Is that the dress?

MONA: What do you think?

FARAH: It looks great. So look, I don't have much time, but I have to say something. I felt awful about turning away from you in the shop after the whole school thing. I mean it's hard being around you sometimes. I mean I love you, but this... religion of yours... It's a tough thing. But I made a decision: no matter what, from now on, I'm going to stick by you, okay?

MONA: (*Wants to believe her.*) Okay.

FARAH: (*Breathes out.*) Good, I think I forgot some of the things I was going to say—so how did you finally get the dress?

MONA: How did you get it is my question? What did you have to pay that guy? I mean, I'll pay you back.

FARAH: I don't know what you mean.

MONA: Don't play. You bought the dress and left it at my door.

FARAH: I did?

ARAM *has entered and stands at a distance. He is drawing in his notebook with considerable care.*

MONA: Didn't you?

FARAH: Maybe. Will you be mad if I didn't?

MONA: No.

FARAH: Then I didn't.

MONA: So who did? No one else was there... (*She turns to look at* ARAM.) Oh no.

FARAH: What? Hey isn't that the guy?

MONA: Yes.

FARAH: What, you think he bought you the dress?

MONA: (*Turns away from him and collapses some under the idea.*) Oh now it makes sense.

FARAH: But who is he? Has he talked to you?

MONA: No, he's following me, but he hasn't said anything. Now I'm wearing his gift he probably thinks we're engaged.

FARAH: Are you going to give it back?

MONA: (*Torn.*) I have to.

FARAH: (*Looks over at* ARAM.) He's pretty good looking.

MONA: Farah!

FARAH: What? Your God is the one who set you two up!

MONA: I've got to get this off. Can you go ask him?

FARAH: What?

MONA: If he gave it to me.

FARAH: Uh...

MONA: I have to know.

FARAH: Fine, but I have to go right after.

MONA: Go, go.

FARAH: All right. (*She approaches* ARAM.) Hey, do you know anything about this dress?

ARAM: (*Holds up his hand and walks away.*) Sorry.

FARAH: Hey, come back, I just want... (*Returning to* MONA.) He walked away.

MONA: What kind of lover is that?

FARAH: I've got to go, but I'm serious about what I said, okay?

They kiss each other on the cheek, and FARAH *leaves.* MONA *looks off the way* ARAM *exited. She slips out of sight. A moment later,* ARAM *enters, looking around for her. He writes something in his notebook.* MONA *sneaks up on him and grabs the notebook, startling him.*

MONA: Who are you and why are you following me?

ARAM: Give it back.

MONA *has retreated so that a tree or a bench is between them.* ARAM *tries to walk around, but she evades him.*

MONA: Don't make me look in your book.

ARAM: Don't.

MONA: (*Reads from his book.*) "I follow wherever you go, Til the light is spent. But then who needs eyes? I'll follow your scent."

ARAM: You have no right to read that.

MONA: (*Relieved, still evading.*) So you're a poet. And an artist?

Some photographs and papers have fallen out of the notebook. MONA *bends to pick them up.*

ARAM: Just leave those!

MONA *picks up a photograph and looks. Lights come up on* EHSAN *just as when he was being executed.*

MONA: Why do you have Ehsan's picture? (*Realization. Gunfire.*) You killed him.

ARAM: Give me that back.

MONA *drops the notebook and turns to walk away as if she has encountered a great evil, fighting a nightmare's paralysis.* ARAM *picks up his things.*

ACT I, Scene 11 – Mona's Home

Home now, MONA *has taken off the blue dress as if it was contaminated. She sits on the rug, shivers, wrapped up in a blanket.*

MONA: O God. O God. O God.

Her FATHER *enters.*

FATHER: Mona? Honey, what's going on?

MONA: (*Covering up.*) I'm fine. (*Heaving in fear or with tears.*) I'm just cold.

FATHER: Hey, what happened? (*No response.*) Come on, talk to me.

MONA: He's a guard.

FATHER: Who?

MONA: (*Nods, and shivers.*) I think he killed Ehsan.

She throws her arms around her FATHER *and starts to sob, really sob.*

FATHER: What is this?

MONA: O God, Daddy, I don't want to lose you.

FATHER: (*Tries to comfort her.*) Come, come. Hey, I'm still here.

MONA: But you don't know! There might be someone following you too.

FATHER: My dear, someone's been following me for years.

MONA: See! Dad, this isn't funny. We should go now, get out of Shiraz, stay with friends until this passes.

FATHER: (*Listening attentively.*) We could.

MONA: Yes, we could.

He looks at her lovingly.

MONA: So?

FATHER: So who would take care of those who can't leave? Who would visit them and comfort them, bring them word about the good things their Bahá'í brothers and sisters are doing around the world? They live for that.

MONA: So you need to die for it?

FATHER: Honey...

MONA: Do it for me if you won't do it for yourself!

FATHER: What can I say? My life is His, and He can take me.

MONA: So you want to die?

FATHER: No. But part of our Faith demands we change our attitude towards death. It is not the end, and we shouldn't fear it as such. What does Bahá'u'lláh say, "I have made death a messenger of joy to thee. Wherefore dost thou grieve?" So don't grieve, my sweet. (*Hugs her as she starts to break again.*) If it were mine to choose, you think I wouldn't want to be part of your life and see you grow and learn and flourish and marry?

MONA: (*Softly.*) But you can, can't you?

He doesn't answer.

MONA: (*Shaking her head.*) We just want to help, but these people— They have no souls.

FATHER: No, no, no, Mona. They have the very same soul, and the same possibility in their lives. Believe that, see that they are your sisters and brothers, but that they are in grave danger, moral danger.

MONA: It's one thing if they put themselves in danger, it's another if they put us, YOU, in danger.

FATHER: Do you think it's an accident that they target us? Or it's just because we're weak and an easy scapegoat? (*Shakes his head.*) We're a direct threat to them.

MONA: What?

FATHER: They're devoting every ounce of their might to forging a world with an imbalance of power, governed by fear, fueled by prejudice, fostered in a climate of ignorance. If there were no clash...

MONA: We wouldn't be doing our work.

FATHER: This is the test, isn't it? (*Pause.*) The world can change, but it will need some of us to stand and point the way.

MONA: So you can't leave.

FATHER: Don't despair. And don't lose hope in people. Transformation can happen to anyone, at any moment. So find the light in each one. Then you will rise from a creature of the earth to be a heavenly being. Then you will be a true Bahá'í.

ACT I, Scene 12 – The Ruins of the House of the Báb

MONA *stands straight and faces forward, with* FARAH *beside her. Both wear head scarves. The arches of a mosque are behind them.* ARAM *is there, and he looks anxious.*

MONA: You're sure you want to do this? Someone over here might come after us.

FARAH: (*Anxious.*) Why are we here again?

MONA: I come when I need strength. This is the House of the Báb. This is where my Faith began.

FARAH: I don't see what's controversial. There's nothing here.

MONA: Why else would they knock it down and leave no trace? (*Slight pause.*) Ready?

FARAH: (*Referring to* ARAM.) What about the guy?

MONA: He can come in if he'd like.

MONA *holds* FARAH*'s hand, closes her eyes a moment, and when she reopens them, she takes a step forward, toward the audience.*

ARAM: Hey!

MONA: He spoke.

ARAM: (*More quietly.*) You shouldn't go in there.

MONA: Go report me if you want.

MONA *walks in, followed by* FARAH. ARAM *is not pleased, and he walks off so as not to see what they are doing.*

MONA: So, in the front here was a wall about this tall—like those houses over there—with a door about here. There is a courtyard with the orange tree right there. (*Moving into the audience with* FARAH.) Windows all around, and a second floor with a flat roof. Up there with all the stained glass is the most important spot, where it all began.

MONA *seems to be seeing all she describes, but* FARAH'*s focus is on her friend, who seems to be changing before her very eyes.*

ACT I, Scene 13 – Mona's Home

Mona's MOTHER *sews distractedly. A knock.*

MOTHER: (*Anxiously stands.*) Come in.

MRS. KHUDAYAR: (*Opens the door, points to a newly-installed peephole.*) What is this, a peephole?

MOTHER: (*As if she's forgotten.*) Oh, in case someone comes. Some friends were just here, Jamshid let them install it—I guess to make them feel better.

MRS. KHUDAYAR: You should turn it around so I can see what's going on inside.

MOTHER: Yes, maybe.

MRS. KHUDAYAR: That was a joke. Look at you worried to death: What can I do?

MOTHER: What can anyone do? They're down there now begging him to go into hiding. There are rumors of arrests—My throat.

MRS. KHUDAYAR: We thought with the Shah gone, it would be freedom for everyone.

MOTHER: (*Sipping her tea.*) Excuse me for drinking.

MRS. KHUDAYAR: You know? I'm thirsty too.

MOTHER: I would offer…

MRS. KHUDAYAR: Okay.

The MOTHER *looks at her surprised.* MRS. KHUDAYAR *nods, though a bit uncertainly. The* MOTHER *then exits to the kitchen.*

MRS. KHUDAYAR: When they come, they're going to trash this place. What if I took your rug and some other things... to hide?

MOTHER: (*Enters, with tea.*) You don't need to do that.

MRS. KHUDAYAR: I insist.

MRS. KHUDAYAR *takes the cup. The* MOTHER *watches it go to her lips where it stops.*

MRS. KHUDAYAR: Always they told me your tea was a magic potion. (*A slight pause.*) Please let me take some of your things.

MOTHER: Okay.

MRS. KHUDAYAR *takes a sip, and then pauses.*

MOTHER: Well?

MRS. KHUDAYAR: Well, I'm disappointed. It's just tea.

They laugh.

MRS. KHUDAYAR: Come on, let me get that son of mine to help in here.

ACT I, Scene 14 – The Mulla's Office

ARAM *is getting grilled by the* MULLA. GUARD 1 *watches.*

MULLA: But why didn't you report it yourself?

ARAM *is quiet.*

MULLA: Why did I have to hear that the girl and her friend were walking on that damned spot by someone else? That's why I have you! To tell me what they're doing. Not to make me look like an idiot when the guy who sits by the shoes and helps wash people's feet knows more about what the Bahá'ís are doing than I do! What do you have to say for yourself?

ARAM: I didn't think it was that important.

MULLA: It's not your place to think what's important. It's your place to come to me with everything you see and then I decide for you what is and what is not important! Got it?

ARAM *doesn't speak.*

MULLA: Now go get the truck, you've got a busy night tonight.

He exits. GUARD 1 *stops* ARAM *from leaving.*

GUARD 1: You know what this guy can do to you?

ACT I, Scene 15 – A Street near Mona's Home

It's evening. FARAH *is latched onto* MONA'*s arm, and they now walk silently, knowing they need to part ways.*

FARAH: I'm not letting go. I'm worried.

MONA: Why?

FARAH: Sorry, all my friends have guard escorts.

MONA: (*Looking back.*) He seems to be gone. It's my father. They don't usually target women, much less girls like me—Don't be sad.

She squishes FARAH'*s cheeks into a smile, but it doesn't stay.*

FARAH: You're changing, aren't you?

MONA: What do you mean?

FARAH: I just feel like you're starting to float away from me.

MONA: I'll always be here with you.

FARAH: Promise?

MONA: (*Smiles, looks up at the sky.*) Pick a star. (*Pause.*) See that bright star near the moon. Look at it and I'm right there with you.

FARAH *points to a star lower on the horizon.*

MONA: Good, that's yours for me.

They hug and part ways.

ACT I, Scene 16 – Mona's Home

The MOTHER *looks about the room that is now missing the rug and a couple of other things. The* FATHER *is then heard off stage talking to* MRS. KHUDAYAR.

FATHER: (*Off.*) Thank you so much, Thank you. I'm sorry, we'll just keep these things in here.

MRS. KHUDAYAR: (*Off, overlapping.*) I insist. Really, it's better we keep them.

MONA *enters, looking down the hall at her* FATHER *and* MRS. KHUDAYAR *playing tug of war.*

MONA: What's going on?

The MOTHER *shakes her head. The* FATHER *enters with the rug and the couple of others things.*

MOTHER: She was trying to be kind. (*Stopping him.*) She drank some of our tea.

FATHER: So?

MOTHER: So the peephole didn't help us either. I thought you'd be proud of me.

MRS. KHUDAYAR: (*Entering.*) It's no problem.

MOTHER: It's just a rug…

FATHER: (*To his wife, at once gentle and firm.*) You think I care about the rug?

MONA *watches, in awe of her* FATHER *whose behavior is difficult to gauge sometimes.* REZA *is now at the door.*

FATHER: Let's say, just hypothetically, that Reza here were to ask for the hand of a girl like, say, Mona.

MONA *and* REZA *are both embarrassed by this.*

MRS. KHUDAYAR: I've told him to get it out of his head—he's not good enough for you.

REZA: Mom!

FATHER: For example—and if he brought a beautiful engagement ring, just right: would he skimp on the box? It might cost a little extra.

MRS. KHUDAYAR: He better not—cheapskate.

FATHER: (*Takes his wife and daughter in his arms.*) These are my diamonds, and our home and everything in it is just a box.

MRS. KHUDAYAR: Of course.

REZA: (*Leaving, to his mother.*) Why do you have to embarrass me like that?

MRS. KHUDAYAR *exits after him. The* FATHER *goes into the kitchen.*

MOTHER: I don't understand that man. Just when I think I do, he goes and changes all the rules on me. And I feel like a child. (*Turning to* MONA.) Even if they do come and arrest him, even if the worst comes. We'll be strong and we'll get through this, okay? If we stay united, we can do it, honey.

MONA *comforts her* MOTHER. *Her* FATHER *has been watching this exchange from the doorway. He solemnly and gratefully nods and steps back out of sight.*

MOTHER: You hungry?

MONA *nods. The* MOTHER *exits into the kitchen and passes by the* FATHER, *who now enters with a plate of food.*

FATHER: My dear, I didn't greet you properly. (*Kisses her and makes to share the plate with her.*)

MONA: You look tired.

FATHER: Thank you. You look radiant.

MONA: I should, I was at the House of the Báb.

FATHER: Mmmm. One day we'll rebuild. If not in my lifetime, then in yours.

MONA: Dad, you might just grow old in this world, and that way, you'll have to take better care of yourself. When I finish school this year, maybe we can look at colleges in other places. We can go to Africa, or America. What do you think?

FATHER: Have an olive.

He puts it in her mouth. A moment of tenderness before MONA *exits. The* MOTHER *has entered and sits beside her husband, affectionately close.*

MOTHER: Maybe she's right. You remember when the girls were young how we used to move so often, and every time you would go ahead and prepare the house, and you'd dress up in your best clothes and come and wait for me. And I'd arrive and you'd usher me in like a queen.

FATHER: I remember each time.

MOTHER: Maybe we'll do that again someday.

FATHER: No thanks.

They laugh. There is a sudden pounding on the door. MONA *is still offstage. Whirling in confusion, the* MOTHER *moves to the door.*

MOTHER: Maybe someone... just... has a question or something. Who is it?

GUARD: (*Off.*) Revolutionary Guard, open up!

MOTHER: (*Hushed.*) Oh, no!

The FATHER *closes his eyes and prepares himself.*

MRS. KHUDAYAR: (*Off.*) They're not home. Why don't you come back later?

MOTHER: It's Mrs. Khudayar...

GUARD 1: (*Off.*) Oh, I think they are home.

MRS. KHUDAYAR: (*Off.*) I saw them go out

One of the GUARDS *begin to force his weight against the door.*

MOTHER: I should have used the peephole! What do I do now?

FATHER: (*Rising.*) Open the door and let them in.

The MOTHER *puts on a dark chador and opens the door as the* FATHER *joins her. He is shaking slightly.*

FATHER: Good evening, friends. What can I do for you?

GUARD 2: We are from the Revolutionary Court. We have a warrant to enter.

GUARD 2 *hands him the warrant. The* FATHER *looks at it.*

FATHER: Please come in.

GUARDS 1 *and* 2 *enter brusquely, followed by* ARAM. *He looks around, surprised not to see* MONA.

GUARD 2: (*To* FATHER.) You sit there, (*To* MOTHER.) And you over there.

GUARD 1: Just you two? (*To* ARAM.) Check for the girl.

ARAM *looks, then* MONA *enters from the bathroom.*

MONA: You.

ARAM: Please go sit on the couch.

MOTHER: Mona, come sit.

GUARD 2: You be quiet.

MONA: I need to cover my hair. (*Moves towards her room.*)

GUARD 2: Come here, girl.

ARAM: Just go and sit down.

MONA: You are not my father and you're not my brother, so I have to cover my hair in your presence.

MONA *goes and gets a scarf around her hair, and retrieves a book.* ARAM *waits.*

GUARD 1: (*Looking through the father's papers.*) Get her out here, we don't have all night!

MONA *comes out, and* GUARD 2 *goes in and closes the door.*

ARAM: (*Low, to* MONA.) Sorry.

MONA *goes to the couch. Just then,* MRS. KHUDAYAR *pushes open the door.* REZA *follows sheepishly behind.*

MRS. KHUDAYAR: Excuse me?

ARAM: Hey, I need some backup in here!

MRS. KHUDAYAR: No trouble, I just want to help.

GUARD 2: Go back to your home!

MRS. KHUDAYAR: Sure, but maybe while you're searching, I can take them too.

GUARD 2: They are unclean!

MRS. KHUDAYAR: They're good people!

GUARD 2: Get out of here!

MRS. KHUDAYAR: Maybe I'm Bahá'í too!

GUARD 2: You don't know the first thing about it!

MRS. KHUDAYAR: How do you know?

GUARD 2: Because I read your mail and listen to your phone calls.

FATHER: (*Rising.*) Thank you so much. We'll let you know when they're done.

GUARD 1: What's going on? (*To* FATHER.) You sit down until we're ready. (*To* MRS. KHUDAYAR.) You, you want your son to go fight in Iraq?

GUARD 2 *levels his gun at* REZA, *who begins to tremble.*

MRS. KHUDAYAR: God no.

GUARD 1: Go home and lock the door.

MRS. KHUDAYAR *obeys, exits with* REZA. GUARD 1 *gives* ARAM *a look.*

GUARD 1: (*To* ARAM.) What's wrong with you?

ARAM: She just walked in.

GUARD 1: No one moves.

MOTHER: (*Shivering.*) Jamshid, they're going to take you.

The FATHER *has his eyes closed.* MONA *has a textbook open, but she's not reading it.* GUARDS 1 *and* 2 *overturn everything.* GUARD 2 *brings in a plastic bag full of Mona's writings and tapes.*

GUARD 1: We've got what we need. (*To* FATHER.) You and the girl, you're coming with us.

FATHER: The girl?

MONA: Me?

FATHER: But why?

MOTHER: You've got to be kidding.

GUARD 1: We're not kidding.

MONA *stands with a mixture of shock and honor.* ARAM *grabs a black chador from a book for* MONA, *but the* MOTHER *stops him.*

MOTHER: If you want to take my husband, okay! But Mona is just a child.

GUARD 2: The things she's writing? These tapes of her voice? They could set the world on fire.

GUARD 1: He means that she could lead others into the fire of ignorance.

MOTHER: All right then, take me instead!

MONA: Mom, calm down.

GUARD 2: Woman, we don't want you.

MOTHER: (*To* ARAM.) Swear to God you won't take her! You won't take her!

MONA: Mom, why are you begging them? I'm not a criminal. They're taking me because of my belief. (*To* GUARD 2.) I'll get my coat.

She goes into her destroyed room. Her FATHER *speaks to his wife.*

FATHER: Farkhundih. (*Looking into the men's faces.*) These men. I love these brothers like my own sons. I am sure it is the will of God that they are here now to take Mona and myself away with them. Just leave everything in God's hands and don't worry about Mona. These brothers look on Mona as their own sister.

The GUARDS *are taken in by this. The* FATHER *indicates he is ready and walks out with* GUARD 1. GUARD 2 *has thrown books, papers and photo albums on top of the carpet, and he rolls it up, indicating to* ARAM *to grab the other side.* ARAM *waits though on* MONA, *who has reentered with her coat.*

MOTHER: You look like a queen.

The MOTHER *takes the black veil from* ARAM *and helps* MONA *put it on. It wraps around and covers up all her color.*

MOTHER: (*Imploring* ARAM.) Tell me you won't take her. Ask the one in charge. No one will notice if she's doesn't go. She's just a girl...

GUARD 2 *is dragging the filled carpet off by himself. Only when he's gone does* ARAM *speak—quietly, dejectedly.*

ARAM: I'm sorry. There's nothing I can do.

MONA: (*Reassuring her* MOTHER.) Mom, it won't be a prison for me, but an open field, a mountain top where I can touch the moon. Please don't worry. We'll see you soon.

She kisses her MOTHER *and, as she goes to leave, she pulls out the blue dress and pushes it into* ARAM*'s hands without looking at him.* ARAM *then closes the door on the* MOTHER, *who is left alone.*

End of Act I

ACT II

Scene 1 – Prison; an interrogation room

MONA *stands blindfolded. She is refusing to answer questions in an interrogation led by* GUARD 2.

GUARD 2: Tired yet?

MONA *doesn't answer, but it's clear she is tired. She remains standing while the scene shifts to* FARAH, *who reads a letter from Mona in front of class. This is a bold move for* FARAH *and for the* TEACHER to allow it.

FARAH: "I put my trust in God to get this letter to you—and in Mínú who is smuggling it out! We're not supposed to write anything except for all the forms they try to get us to fill out. Forty Bahá'ís, both men and women, were arrested the same night. From what I can gather, I'm the youngest. But don't worry too much about me, I have a wonderful family here with my fellow women prisoners, both Bahá'ís and Muslims. (The Muslims call me 'little prisoner.') Last night, I felt as though I were on a balcony getting closer to the moon, but I kept seeing my mother's face. Farah, please go see her, and my sister and little Nura, and hug and kiss them for me. They visit, but there's a barrier between us. As for my father, I have only seen him once since coming here."

Scene shift away from the classroom and back to the Interrogation room. MONA*'s legs are asleep, and she winces to shake them out.*

GUARD 2: Answer me and I'll let you sit. Describe your Bahá'í activities.

No response.

GUARD 2: We can arrange your release.

Still no response.

GUARD 2: Look, I know this is more your parents' religion than yours.

ARAM *has entered and whispers to* GUARD 2.

GUARD 2: So what if I brought your father in here to persuade you to talk to me? (*Getting close.*) But you know your father wouldn't do that, right?

He nods to ARAM, *who exits.*

GUARD 2: He took many days, but since then, he's been quite useful to us.

MONA: You'll never break my father.

GUARD 2: No? I just broke you.

MONA *clams up. Mona's* FATHER *is wheeled in, blindfolded, ravaged by torture, having been whipped constantly on the back and on the feet. When he speaks, it's with a soft, strained voice.*

GUARD 2: Mahmudnizhad, your daughter is here.

FATHER: Mona dear?

MONA: Dad?

GUARD 2: Stay where you are. Tell her.

FATHER: Answer their questions, honey.

MONA *doesn't know how to respond.*

FATHER: Tell them what they want to know, Mona. Tell them the truth.

MONA: Dad, what have they done to you?

GUARD 2: You want to see?

YOUNG MAN: (*Quietly.*) Wait.

GUARD 2: What?

ARAM *objects, showing some backbone.*

GUARD 2: What, are you going soft? (*Continuing.*) Fine, just imagine the soles of his feet being struck with a rod time and again as the pain shoots up the body into the brain...

FATHER: (*Overlapping.*) You don't need to share this.

GUARD 2: Oh I do. You see it's cleaner than the back lashes, because you know it takes several days for the feet to start to bleed. But when they do, they bleed from the nails.

MONA: What makes you people so sick?

GUARD 2: See, you've got it upside down. You are sick, and we resort to these means to cure you!

FATHER: Mona, after a while I don't feel the pain.

MONA: But the agreement!

A beat, while the FATHER *gathers the strength to speak.*

FATHER: We have no secrets, Mona. Our activities are not political, and we are faithful to our country.

GUARD 2: So your world center in Israel isn't political!

FATHER: (*Matter-of-factly.*) You exiled our Prophet there a hundred years ago, locked Him in a stone fortress. Where else is our world center going to be?

GUARD 2: (*To* ARAM.) Hit him!

ARAM: You want me to get 'Abdu'llah?

GUARD 2: No I want you to hit him.

MONA: Don't.

GUARD 2: Shut up! It's either him or her.

MONA: Me then.

FATHER: Please.

MONA: (*To* ARAM.) You can stand up to them—tell them this is not the way of Islam.

GUARD 2: Don't tell me about Islam. (*To* ARAM, *as if it's his last chance.*) Hit him or I tell the Magistrate.

ARAM *picks up the whip, and then picks up the Qur'an, which lies open. He puts the book under his arm (a practice employed to limit the force of the lashes).*

GUARD 2: What are you doing?

ARAM: To get the right amount of force.

GUARD 2: This man is an apostate—you hit him like this, this is going to save him from the fires of hell?!

ARAM: Okay!

ARAM *begins to whip the* FATHER's *back.* MONA *is torn.*

FATHER: Mmmm.

GUARD 2: Harder! Girl?

Another lash.

FATHER: Aaaah!

GUARD 2: Again, harder! GIIRRLL?

Another lash.

FATHER: Yá Bahá'u'l-abhá![3]

MONA: STOP!

GUARD 2: Are you going to talk?!

MONA: (*After a pause.*) Let me see his eyes...

GUARD 2 *senses victory and motions to* ARAM, *who pulls up his mask, then takes off their blindfolds.* MONA *goes to her* FATHER.

MONA: Oh Dad! Look at you …

FATHER: Is it really you?

MONA: What have they done?

FATHER: Don't look there—let me see you.

They look in each other's eyes.

GUARD 2: Tell her.

---

[3] An invocation meaning "O Glory of the Most Glorious" in Arabic. (See Glossary)

FATHER: Answer them bravely and honestly. We have nothing to hide.

MONA *hesitates.*

GUARD 2: Quick, quick.

FATHER: Tell the women to see their captors not as enemies but as friends, with whom they can share their love.

MONA: What?

GUARD 2: He thinks he's going to convert us!

MONA: But is that right?

FATHER: Do I look like I have any secrets left?

A beat in which MONA *seems to assent.*

GUARD 2: Let me get the Magistrate.

He exits. MONA *looks at her father's wounds.*

MONA: They're not friends. They're devils.

FATHER: Don't hate them. Don't even be angry with them.

ARAM *is there.*

MONA: (*Gives him an evil look.*) Leave us alone.

ARAM: Sir, I'm sorry.

FATHER: Son, it was more painful for you.

ARAM *is moved.* MONA *is livid.*

MONA: How can you say that?

ARAM: (*Still to* FATHER.) I'm going to make sure she's released, okay?

MONA: I don't want anything from you, just stay away!

FATHER: Love, Mona. Only love.

MONA *is speechless, unable to fathom this depth.* ARAM *starts to push the* FATHER *out one of the doors. In a vision,* MONA *sees the* WOMAN IN WHITE *at the door, radiant, watching the* FATHER *wheeled off. Then, the door opposite opens and fire seems to pour in.* MONA *hides her face just as the* MULLA *enters. He looks at* MONA *curiously.*

MULLA: Where's her blindfold?

GUARD 2: She has all the forms to answer.

MONA *has opened her eyes, but she keeps her gaze averted.*

MULLA: (*To* MONA.) Sweetheart, we're going to let you go. Don't worry, we just need you to do a little paperwork.

He looks her over and raises his eyebrows to GUARD 2. *He then walks out.* GUARD 2 *hands* MONA *a stack of papers and a pen. The air returns to the room and she settles in to the burden of paperwork.*

ACT II, Scene 2 – A Prison Office

TARANEH *and* MOTHER *approach the front entrance to the prison.* TARANEH *carries a baby girl, little* NURA. *The* MOTHER *has Mona's release paper in her hand.*

MOTHER: I'm telling you there are no gas stations out here.

TARANEH: We'll walk back! I'm not going to miss getting Mona.

MOTHER: It's not a sure thing they'll release her, form or no form.

TARANEH: (*Bangs on the door.*) Hello, we have a visit scheduled! (*To* MOTHER.) So you have the money?

MOTHER: (*Referring to baby.*) I can't believe the way she slept.

TARANEH: She's used to Mommy's driving. The Assembly agreed to the bond, right? (*Bangs on the door again.*) Hey, it's one o'clock!

The MOTHER *appears not to have heard her question.*

TARANEH: Mom?

MOTHER: Sorry, I can't concentrate now. I'm so worried about them both.

TARANEH: (*Suspicious, takes the paper from her* MOTHER.) So first we visit with Mona and then they release her? That doesn't make sense.

MOTHER: (*Hands on her kidneys.*) Aaaeeeee.

GUARD 1 *comes to open the door.*

MOTHER: Is it possible to come in? I'd like to freshen up before my visit, you understand.

GUARD 1: Just you.

MOTHER: This is her sister.

GUARD 1: She needs to wait outside.

TARANEH: Go ahead, Mom. I'll... I'll just wait out here.

She hands the release to her MOTHER *and walks off with the baby. The* MOTHER *is ushered into an office by* GUARD 1.

GUARD 1: It'll be another minute.

MOTHER: Is it possible to freshen up before my visit, you understand?

GUARD 1: It'll just be a minute.

He is gone. She tries to sit.

MOTHER: (*Hands on her kidneys.*) Ooohhhhhh. (*She is back up.*) O God, I want my child. I want Mona from you. I want to touch her, to kiss her cheek. The little birds all fly free but my little bird is trapped in a cage. O God, we need a miracle. Bring her to me.

The MULLA *enters.*

MULLA: Please sit.

MOTHER: Please, is there a rest room?

MULLA: I'll make this quick if you will.

ARAM *enters.*

MULLA: Where's the girl's file?

ARAM *has forgotten this, and exits, embarrassed. The* MOTHER *goes to hand the release paper to the* MULLA.

MULLA: So what was it, 100,000 Tuman?

MOTHER: (*Hesitates with the form.*) Something like that—

MULLA: (*Overlapping, snatching the form from her.*) It was 200, I remember.

MOTHER: Can I see her now?

MULLA: Can I see the money?

MOTHER: There is concern if we pay 200,000 now, tomorrow it might be 400, the next day 600.

MULLA: You think I'm going to cheat you?

MOTHER: Not me, if it were just me...

MULLA: Who then? The Bahá'í Assembly?

MOTHER: You're twisting my words.

ARAM *reenters with a thick stack of papers.*

MULLA: (*To* ARAM.) It's all here?

ARAM *nods.*

MULLA: And where is she?

ARAM: She's in a holding room, just down the hall here.

MOTHER: She's right here. Please let me see her. Just say you won't increase bail, I'll pay you in 24 hours.

A beat. The MULLA *calculates.*

MULLA: (*To* ARAM.) Send the girl back to her cell. (*Hands* ARAM *the release form. To* MOTHER.) Now I have some questions for you.

Flustered, ARAM *goes into the hall and he lingers there, looks at the form. The* MOTHER *is disbelieving.*

MULLA: Who made this decision about the bail?

MOTHER: What more do you need from me? You have my husband, you have my daughter. Maybe I have a few questions for you.

MULLA: I want names.

MOTHER: I'm not your prisoner.

MULLA: No?

He impulsively takes a stamp and brings it down on a legal form, then signs it.

MULLA: Now you're my prisoner. (*Gets up to go.*) You think you can toy with me, woman.

He walks out to the hall and sees ARAM *there. The* MOTHER *is aghast.*

MULLA: (*Impatient.*) What?

ARAM: (*Holding Mona's release.*) You said you want me to put her back in her cell?

MULLA: You want to toy with me too, boy? (*Tears the release in two, tosses it in the air.*) No, no, no, this is all going to change!

He exits. ARAM *picks up the torn release form. Seeing the devastated* MOTHER, *he follows after the Mulla, stealthily, as if to spy on him.*

ACT II, Scene 3 – A Prison Holding Room

MONA *waits. The sound of screaming from doors down. The door opens; it's* ARAM. *He looks around, makes a judgment, shuts the door and locks it.*

MONA: (*Nervous.*) A woman needs to be here.

ARAM: We need to talk.

MONA: Am I being released?

ARAM: No.

MONA: Then take me to my cell.

ARAM: I just overheard something: he's going to start executing women.

MONA *sits. He takes out a pen and the torn release, which he has taped.*

MONA: What's that for?

ARAM: If you just write down a few sentences, I think they'll let you go.

MONA: Please take me back to my cell.

ARAM: It's just a piece of paper. (*A beat.*) Look, I've been watching you, and your father, and others. I know it's not right. I know you're good people. But if you let them do this, out of pride or spite or whatever it is that makes you people so stubborn, you are responsible, Mona.

A beat.

MONA: (*Still cold.*) What's your name?

ARAM: Aram.

MONA: (*Maybe not fully believing.*) If they kill us, Aram, God will raise up others greater than us.

ARAM: You don't know that.

MONA: I do. That's how it works.

Someone bangs on the door. ARAM *jumps back behind where the door would open.*

ARAM: (*Whispers.*) Hide.

MONA *doesn't. Someone checks the door, finds it locked, and passes.* ARAM *comes back to the table.*

ARAM: You had a dream, with the dresses.

MONA: (*Defenses rising.*) You read my file?

ARAM: (*Not flinching.*) Doesn't it make sense that I am here in front of you, apparently chosen by God, to remind you what He has chosen for you? Not death, not suffering, but life.

ARAM *has written something on the paper and pushes it towards her.*

MONA: (*Reading.*) "I renounce my membership in the Bahá'í Faith." (*Pauses.*) Here's the truth: I chose the blue dress and I served. I chose the black and I've suffered. As for the red, I don't know if I am ready or worthy, but if you're the face I saw, it's not because you're chosen of God, but it's that, despite the terrible, terrible things you've done, I have to stop hating you!

She rips up the release paper and throws it in the air.

ARAM: Terrible things like what?

MONA: Like killing Ehsan, Mr. Khushkhu, and Mr. Vahdat.

ARAM: No. Your friend, he kissed my hand. I couldn't fire, but I watched him die, like a hero, and now he haunts me every waking moment, following me wherever I go. I never killed anyone.

ARAM *doesn't see that the door has been opened, and the* MULLA *stands, keys in hand, listening to all this.*

MULLA: Is that right?

ACT II, Scene 4 – Outside the Prison

TARANEH *bangs on the same door as before, little* NURA *sleeping in her arms. She bangs harder.* GUARD 1 *comes out.*

GUARD 1: We're closed.

TARANEH: Sorry, I've been waiting for my mother. Do you know where she is?

GUARD 1: No. Come back tomorrow. (*Goes to leave.*)

TARANEH: I don't have enough gas to get home, my mother has our cash. Can you go back inside and ask for her?

GUARD 1: No.

He leaves. TARANEH *is stunned.*

TARANEH: (*To sleeping daughter.*) What do we do now, sweetie? (*A beat.*) I was in such a rush.

GUARD 1 *reenters. He opens the door, pushes some money (5 tuman) into her hand, then goes.*

TARANEH: Thank you—God.

ACT II, Scene 5 – Prison Courtyard

It's night. MONA *and several other women are blindfolded in a staggered line. The* MULLA *is there with a machine gun in his hand as he remonstrates with* ARAM. GUARD 2 *is nearby with a gun of his own.*

MULLA: So why the Revolutionary Guard, Hafez, if you lack the constitution for it? And be honest, a general needs to know where his soldiers stand.

ARAM: I preferred Shiraz to Iraq.

MULLA: Well, that's honest. Shiraz sure beats Iraq! (*Laughs.*) Yeah, but you know, wherever you go, God will find you out. (*Hands him the gun. Speaks to* GUARD 2.) Get 'em lined up.

GUARD 2: Prisoners! Line up, and stand up straight!

The MULLA *nods and* GUARD 2 *raises his gun, aiming at the women.* ARAM *hesitates to do the same, so the* MULLA *indicates to* GUARD 2 *to level his gun at* ARAM. ARAM *raises his gun tepidly.*

MULLA: Ladies, you are about to be executed. See if your Bahá'í God saves you now.

Some begin to cry and pray aloud. MONA *squeezes the hand of the woman next to her.*

MONA: God help us.

The MULLA *nods to* ARAM *to fire.* ARAM *can't. Instead* GUARD 2 *begins to fire wildly. Screams and bodies falling and writhing.* ARAM *looks on, stunned, to see perhaps half of the women who remain standing as if nothing has touched them.*

A scene shift where the WOMAN IN WHITE *appears, luminous, as if a protector of these several women. A celestial birdsong.*

The women look around, blindfolds still on. Are they dead? Moaning is heard, then weeping. The cries come mainly from the ones who have fallen. One begins to rage.

WOMAN: We're alive! They didn't shoot—this is just a sick, twisted game!

ARAM *is just as shocked as the women.* GUARD 2 *though was in the know.*

GUARD 2: (*Smiles, to* ARAM.) Aimed over their heads.

ARAM *catches his breath.*

MULLA: They weren't the real target. (*Takes* ARAM*'s gun. To* GUARD 2.) Take the ones on the ground to interrogation. The ones standing, bring them to their cells. (*To* MONA*'s group.*) Congratulations, ladies, you won that round. Miss Mahmudnizhad, you'll be happy to know your mother will be waiting for you.

MONA: My mother?

She and the other are ushered off. The MULLA *and* ARAM *are left.*

MULLA: (*With a mixture of admiration and impatience.*) See that? When they don't fear death any more, we start to run out of options. And then there are things worse than death, right, Hafez?

ACT II, Scene 6 – Prison Cell & Visitation Area

MONA *is brought to her cell with* WOMAN 2, *one of those who remained standing in the previous scene. Their blindfolds are removed.*

MONA: Did you see it?

WOMAN 2 *nods in wonder.*

MONA: It was like a world of love and light opening up to us. I don't know why we're still here.

They comfort each other. Her MOTHER *is brought in. She is layered with blankets.* WOMAN 2 *is led off.*

MOTHER: Mona? Is that you?

MONA: Mom?

MOTHER: Oh honey, I love you so much. Oh, let me hug you, let me kiss you!

MONA: What are you doing in here?

MOTHER: They kept me in that room for hours! It was awful. But what's happened to you? Look at you, you're shaking?

MONA: I'm just so happy to see you.

They hold each other tight. Scene shift to the Visitation Area. The FATHER *and* TARANEH *are separated by a glass barrier and they speak through phones.*

TARANEH: You know Mom is in now.

He nods. TARANEH *begins to cry. He shakes his head.*

FATHER: It's not as bad as that.

TARANEH: Dad, I just feel so helpless and alone. I can't seem to do anything to get you released. I try: I go here, they send me there, I go there, they send me right back. I'm depressed and it's not good for the baby, I know. I feel...

FATHER: What?

TARANEH: I feel left out, like God has forgotten me. Wasn't I worth being imprisoned for my Faith too?

FATHER: My dear, you on the outside are in the harsher prison.

TARANEH: (*Nodding, then—*) You mean Iran?

He smiles lovingly. The scene shifts back to the prison cell, where MONA, *her* MOTHER, *and a couple other women sit back to back on the ground.*

MOTHER: Here, honey, take a blanket. I just threw them all on top of me.

MONA: I'm okay. Have you eaten yet?

MOTHER: So cold in here! I don't know how you girls aren't freezing to death.

MONA: Here, Mom, have another blanket. You haven't eaten your dinner.

MOTHER: I don't know who could. And the smell, I can barely breathe.

MONA: You're just not used to it.

MOTHER: You get used to it?

MONA: It's important to keep the right attitude in here—

An obnoxiously loud VOICE *comes over the* P.A. *system.*

VOICE OVER P.A.: Prisoners! A victory for Islam! Last night, a husband and wife, recanted the Bahá'í heresy. Now they are free!

Someone groans. The rest seem to hold their breath.

VOICE OVER P.A.: To celebrate, we are letting family members in prison meet to talk it over.

Reactions. The other women kiss MONA *and her* MOTHER *and exit, as if back to their own cells.*

VOICE OVER P.A.: Islam is the open door!

The FATHER *makes his way, barely able to walk, but* GUARD 2 *helps him. He focuses ahead, trying not to give attention to the great pain, and sees* MONA *and the* MOTHER.

FATHER: Look, look who—Brother, thank you for bringing me this far.

MOTHER: O Lord!

MONA: Daddy!

MOTHER: Look at you, Jamshid. Look at what they've done to you.

Arriving, he shakes GUARD 2*'s shoulders as if to show he is his brother.* MONA *and the* MOTHER *make room for him to sit, and for a while they just look at each other.*

MONA: You look like a candle.

FATHER: Just waiting for His breath to blow.

MOTHER: No, don't say that—you'll still be okay. Jamshid, what will become of me if you go?

FATHER: (*Speaking with difficulty, but with dignity and joy.*) My wife, from Bahá'u'lláh, our inheritance is prison. From the Báb, martyrdom.

MOTHER: Please stop—My heart is breaking.

FATHER: Mine is overflowing.

MONA *rises and kisses her* FATHER*'s eyes. They look at each other and tears are falling.*

FATHER: I'm so happy. These tears are from happiness. This is not goodbye. We have a new home, I am going.

The MOTHER *is overcome, but she nods.*

FATHER: And when the time is right, I will come for you.

MOTHER: I'm going to hold you to that. I'm sorry, I'm so sorry …

FATHER: No, no. All is washed clean.

MOTHER: Please no more. Talk to Mona, you haven't said a word.

He looks into MONA*'s eyes lovingly, searchingly.*

FATHER: Are you heavenly or earthly?

MONA: Heavenly.

FATHER: (*Standing with a spurt of energy.*) Then let's go!

Scene shift as if the FATHER *has started his ascent to the next world, embodied by the* WOMAN IN WHITE*'s beckoning.* MONA *sees and speaks to her* FATHER *as if across time, but the* MOTHER *recedes.* GUARD 2 *has entered.*

GUARD 2: Yadu'lláh Mahmúdnizhád.

MONA: Must you go now?

GUARD 2: Rahmatu'lláh Vafáí.

FATHER: This separation is only temporary.

GUARD 2: Túbá Zá'irpúr

MONA: Just a little longer.

WOMAN IN WHITE: Come.

MONA: Wait. What about me?

FATHER: Your dress isn't finished. It should be one color, just one.

MONA: What do you mean?

FATHER: Love, Mona—This is the real color of your dress.

MONA: Daddy...!

The FATHER *goes with the* WOMAN IN WHITE. *We see, if anything, the briefest enactment in silence of the hanging of the three.*

FATHER: (*Just before going.*) May my life be sacrificed for you.

Silence.

MONA: (*Alone, without a tear.*) Won't you congratulate me, friends? My father has been martyred for his faith, and I am so immensely proud of him.

The silence is broken by the scream of the MOTHER, *who wanders just offstage, inconsolable, banging on the bars.*

MOTHER: (*Barely intelligible.*) Where is Mona? Where is my daughter?

MONA: (*Not addressing her directly, still with minimal emotion.*) Mother, I think I need to be alone.

ACT II, Scene 7 – Prison Cell and Elsewhere

It's the next night. MONA *is on the floor of their cell, facing away, praying fervidly. Her* MOTHER, *still grief-stricken, is comforted by other prisoners.*

MOTHER: It's been a full day: she doesn't eat, she doesn't talk. O God, I can't lose her too.

WOMAN: Let her be. Come, Farkhundih, she'll be okay.

They move her off. Elsewhere, FARAH *is searching the sky for Mona's star.*

FARAH: Where are you tonight, Mona? I can't find your star. Are you up there? It's me, Farah. See me, on the horizon—there, at the foot of the bear. I look up, I see the moon, but no Mona nearby. You said you'd be there! Maybe the moon has swallowed you up, swallowed you whole, you made it jealous the way you shine. Can the moon put out the light of a star? No, I know this much: next to a star, a moon is a speck of dust. You'll come back. I'm counting on you to come back.

Scene shift back to MONA. *The prison though has shifted. There's no one around, no sound, and there are hints in the lighting that eternity waits behind these walls.* MONA *stands. She walks to the wall and kicks it.*

MONA: Let me out!

She shouts and hits the walls with her fists and feet.

MONA: (*More in pain than anger.*) I want out. Why don't you take me? You showed me the other side...Why am I still here where one pointless day leads into another unless for some reason? Does my pain mean anything? Does it…

She can't finish the thought. ARAM *is there in the shadows.*

ARAM: Say it.

MONA: (*Startled.*) What are you doing here?

ARAM: (*Finishing* MONA*'s thought.*) Does it please Him to see you in pain?

He has come more into the light; he is a wreck of abuse and wears a mask. He is weak and leans against a wall to keep balance.

ARAM: That's what you can't bring yourself to say.

MONA: You don't belong here.

The crack of a whip and ARAM *buckles. He lurches closer, struggling here and throughout to stand upright.*

MONA: Stop! Stay back!

ARAM: You need to stop!

MONA: (*Pushing back at him.*) Me?! You're threatening me!

Another crack of a whip.

ARAM: (*Falling back from her.*) Look at me!

ARAM *takes off his mask; his face is beaten black and blue. He struggles to stand upright.*

MONA: (*Repulsed.*) Yagghh...

ARAM: Look at what you did!

MONA: I didn't do that. Help!!

The WOMAN IN WHITE *is revealed with several other* SPIRITS.

WOMAN IN WHITE: Aram.

ARAM *goes to her, as if seeking her protection.*

WOMAN IN WHITE: Oooh...

She touches his face and looks to MONA, *who is astonished. Sensing she's being blamed,* MONA *shakes her head "no." The* WOMAN IN WHITE *smiles gently. There is a surging of light from beyond the prison walls. The* WOMAN IN WHITE *and the others turn towards the light.*

MONA: Are you here to take me? To where you are?

WOMAN IN WHITE: I'm here with you.

MONA: But you're not. You're... illumined.

WOMAN IN WHITE: This is the world of light.

There is another surging of light, brighter than before.

MONA: Then why is he here?

The whip again.

ARAM: Stop hurting me!

MONA: (*Advancing on him.*) You're the guard, you're the man—even though you have no spine...

The whip punctuates each statement.

ARAM: (*In agony.*) She's doing it again!

Overcome, he's attended to by the SPIRITS.

MONA: I don't understand.

WOMAN IN WHITE: The rules are different here. (*A beat.*) What is it that you want?

MONA: (*Bracing herself.*) I would like to trade my blue and black dresses for the red.

ARAM: (*Comes up to her.*) No! No! You can't!!

MONA: Do it!

She opens her arms as if bracing for death, but he doesn't touch her. Instead, the WOMAN IN WHITE *does.*

WOMAN IN WHITE: Mona, he can't hurt you here. Here you are strong.

The lights swell again. The MULLA *is wheeled across the back of the stage in a lamentable, comatose state. All turn to watch as mourners would a coffin.*

MONA: (*With awakened anxiety.*) So this is the next world? Why does it look like a prison?

WOMAN IN WHITE: (*Smiles gently.*) Friends...

She motions the SPIRITS *over. They gather around* MONA *as the prisoners had earlier. Silence as they listen.*

SPIRITS: (*Speaking alternately.*) Flowers. Air, fresh air. Sky. Water. Kabab.

They laugh.

SPIRITS: Love. Family. Companionship. Children (*All together.*) Children! (*One by one, again—*) She loves children.

MONA *laughs.*

SPIRITS: Healing. Peace. Freedom. (*Several agree.*) Freedom.

MONA: (*Thrilled but anxious.*) But how is love for flowers or children or freedom bad?

The SPIRITS *resume listening, and only speak with reticence. They do not wish to look at the negative and are careful to mitigate.*

SPIRITS: Some fear. Anger. Often overcome through prayer. Need for justice. Retribution.

MONA: So is it a bad thing to want justice?

No response.

MONA: Come on, look what they've done. (*Moved, tears*) They killed him. O God, they killed him, and now I can't see him anymore unless you let me come here.

SPIRITS: (*So gently.*) Heartbreak.

ARAM: It's despair.

He comes forward. The SPIRITS *do not object, but withdraw from the discussion. This is the darkness.*

ARAM: Despair that you are forgotten. And that even if God is there, He doesn't care about your pain. So to save yourself you kick and scream and flail at the night.

MONA: You see that in me?

ARAM: I see it in everyone. I try to avoid it, but, in my heart, I don't feel Him.

MONA: I do.

ARAM: Even when you look at me? (*A beat.*) God can work through me too, right, Mona? You're so... beyond where I am. If you don't see any hope for me...

He gestures "how can I?" but in such an innocent, childlike way. MONA *breathes in, and there is a crack and the prison walls begin to move. The light starts to shine in.*

ARAM: My father showed you such kindness, and I didn't understand. I saw what you'd done in darkness. He saw who you are, here.

WOMAN IN WHITE: It's time.

MONA: I'm not ready to go back. I don't know if I'll be able to hold onto this.

The vision is nearing an end as the light has reached its peak. ARAM *stands, more sturdily than before. Someone comes forward with a package. It has a red bow.*

WOMAN IN WHITE: What is it that you want?

MONA: (*After a moment.*) Perseverance.

The SPIRITS *gather around.*

WOMAN IN WHITE & SPIRITS: What do you want for yourself from us?

MONA: Perseverance for all the Bahá'ís.

WOMAN IN WHITE: What do you want for yourself from us?

The scene is painfully shifting back to the physical realm, back to the prison cell.

MONA: (*Under the strain of reentry.*) Perseverance, perseverance, perseverance.

WOMAN IN WHITE: We will be watching.

She is gone with her companions. It is now morning. MONA *sits on the bed, bathing in the light of a new day as it pours through an upstage window. Everywhere else is dark.*

The MOTHER *wakens to see* MONA *looking like a vision in light.*

MOTHER: How radiant you are.

MONA *turns and smiles.*

MOTHER: So you're back?

MONA *turns back to the light. The* MOTHER *sits on the bed.*

MOTHER: I've been trying to imagine life without your father, and all I can think of is how I want us to be free and you to have a family.

MONA: I need to tell you something.

MOTHER: Okay.

MONA: I'm going to be executed.

MOTHER: Don't say that.

MONA: Do you want to know how I know?

MOTHER: I don't want to know anything about that!

MONA: If you don't let me tell you, you will regret it later.

MOTHER: O God, you know a mother's heart, you created it and you see it breaking, don't you? Please don't let Mona be executed, please don't—

MONA: Mom, stop.

MOTHER: Look how beautiful you are. You can't see, but my God! If you died, don't you see what a pity it would be?

MONA: That's okay.

MOTHER: But a family! A loving husband! Children!

MONA: (*A discovery:*) Maybe a family is not what I want or need. (*Pauses, more discoveries:*) What I really want is bigger than that. I want to see this world changed, Mom. I want freedom and love and opportunity and joy and light for all the people of the world. And I want the children and the youth to take the lead. If they rose up and overcame the barriers that have separated us, if they learned to meet hatred with love, they could become a new race of men that the world has been waiting for, dying for! The world needs them, desperately, and I believe somehow, if I am strong enough to take this path before me, it will help them on their path. And they'll change this earth into heaven. That's what I want really. That's my dream, Mom. And for that dream, I wish I had a thousand lives to give. (*Pauses.*) Do you see?

The MOTHER *is changed by* MONA*'s vision.*

MOTHER: I do.

MONA *smiles.*

MOTHER: It frightens me, but I do. (*Standing up.*) If only they would come now and take us all!

GUARD 2 *enters.*

GUARD 2: It's time.

ACT II, Scene 8 – Prison Courtroom

A makeshift courtroom. The MULLA *sits at a large table. At the corner are a chair and a typewriter. There is a chair in front of the table meant for the accused.* GUARD 1 *leads the* MOTHER *forward.*

GUARD 1: Wait there, please. (*He takes up a seat before the typewriter.*) Come now.

The MOTHER *comes forward.*

MOTHER: Hello.

GUARD 1 *types it ('hello'). The* MOTHER *goes to the chair but doesn't sit down; instead she stands with her hand on the chair and pretends to be deaf.*

MULLA: Sit down, please.

MOTHER: What's that?

MULLA: Sit down.

MOTHER: Sorry?

MULLA: (*Smiling.*) So now you're deaf? (*To* GUARD 1.) This is the wife of the man who kept saying they have to tell the truth.

He laughs, and goes through her file. The MOTHER *is edified and gives up the deaf pretense.*

MOTHER: Is this all? I've seen courtrooms and hearings at the movies, and there is always a defense attorney and witnesses.

MULLA: This is not the movies! Sit down.

She does.

MULLA: You are from a Zoroastrian background, right?

MOTHER: Yes.

MULLA: Why did you leave such a good religion as the Faith of Zoroaster and convert to Bahá'ísm?

MOTHER: Because it was my heart's desire to do that.

MULLA: This is not a matter of the heart! If right now you declare you are Zoroastrian, I will set you free.

MOTHER: No sir, I will neither become a Zoroastrian nor a Muslim, so what is my sentence?

MULLA: Death.

MOTHER: (*Defiant.*) I am not worthy of martyrdom, but it would make me very happy. As God is my witness, it will make me immeasurably happy.

MULLA: You will be happy?

MOTHER: Yes.

MULLA: We are not here to make you happy! Take her.

The MOTHER *is taken away.* MONA *is brought in. Same business as before.*

MULLA: Your parents have deceived and misled you. They have forced you to imitate them.

MONA: It's true that I was born into it, but I have made up my own mind.

MULLA: Girl, you don't know the first thing about religion.

MONA *raises her gaze, which until now was lowered, and smiles.*

MULLA: Why are you smiling?

MONA: What more proof do you want? You took me out of my parents' home, out of school, brought me to this prison, put me through these interrogation and hardship, you killed my father—what haven't I suffered for my religion.

MULLA: Stop. Stop moving your arms and body like that—you're trying to distract me from my duties! (*A beat.*) What harm did you find in Islam that made you turn away from it?

MONA: I believe in Islam. I also believe that from time to time God renews His religion when it becomes darkened—and so He has sent a new Messenger, Bahá'u'lláh, and He has brought new laws…

MULLA: Muhammad is the Seal of the Prophets—There will be no more Messengers!

MONA: (*Overlapping.*) Now if by Islam you mean the hatred and bloodshed going on in this country, now that is the reason I'm a Bahá'í!

MULLA: Silence! (*Pause.*) We must obey the Qur'an. Accept Islam or face execution.

MONA: (*Moved.*) I kiss the order of execution.

MULLA: Very well, bring the mother back in!

GUARD 1 *exits. A bird is heard singing outside.*

MULLA: You're smiling again!

MONA: The world is waking up.

MULLA: Forget about the world! No one's going to hear what's happened to you here! It all ends right now. We're going to snuff you out—not just you, all of you! Somebody find that bird and kill it.

The MULLA *tries to regain his composure, calculates.* GUARD 1 *returns, leading the* MOTHER *in.* MONA *and her* MOTHER *stand side by side and hold hands in solidarity.*

MULLA: (*To* MOTHER.) Mrs. Mahmúdnizhád, you wanted to know what your sentence was?

MOTHER: Yes.

MULLA: We have killed your husband, we will now kill your daughter. Your sentence is your freedom. You are free to go home and spend the rest of your days mourning their loss.

This was unexpected.

MOTHER: Mona?

MONA: No tears, Mom, remember our talk!

MULLA: Get her out of here!

MOTHER: O my lovely daughter!

The MOTHER *is forced out of the room. The* MULLA *speaks to* GUARD 2, *referring to* MONA.

MULLA: Take her, put her with the other nine. Hang them one at a time from oldest to youngest. This one will be the last. Perhaps the sight of the older ones choking and flailing about will encourage the younger ones.

All are gone. The MULLA *sighs.*

Scene shift to a solitary confinement cell, the size of a dog cage. ARAM *is in it, though we can't recognize him at first. He whines like an animal. The* MULLA *comes up and crouches down.*

MULLA: I have a job for you if you're ready to come out.

He sticks his hand close to the bars, and ARAM *crawls to kiss it.*

ACT II, Scene 9 – An Abandoned Polo Field & Beyond

MONA *stands still, praying.* ARAM *enters, masked, bruised and beaten all over. He approaches* MONA.

ARAM: I don't want to kill you, Mona.

MONA: (*Without looking at him.*) Do your job.

ARAM: (*Takes off his mask.*) I had a vision of you, in my cell.

MONA: I'm sorry.

ARAM: You were nursing my wounds.

Something inside MONA *lets go. She looks up at* ARAM *with great love. Her* FATHER *and the* WOMAN IN WHITE *are now present.* MONA *takes* ARAM*'s hand, which he pulls back, but she gently insists.*

MONA: I see why now. You have made my dream come true.

ARAM: I'll tell them what you've done here.

She kisses his hand and they step upstage. The company comes forward to lay down dresses for each of the 10 women martyrs of Shiraz, as the actor playing the FATHER *reads their names.*

FATHER: 'Izzat Ishráqí. Nusrat Yaldá'í. Táhirih Síyávushí. Zarrín Muqímí. Mahshíd Nírúmand. Shírín Dálvand. Símín Sábirí. Akhtar Sábet. Royá Ishráqí. Mona Mahmúdnizhád.

When called, MONA *comes forward wearing the red dress and lays down her chador as the final dress.*

End of Play

Mona & Yadu'lláh Mahmúdnizhád

SUPPLEMENTARY MATERIALS

The Lover at the Wall
(Excerpts from an Essay)

From the fall of 1982 to mid-June 1983, Mona Mahmudnizhad—the teenaged protagonist of "A New Dress for Mona" and scores of other innocents like her languished behind prison walls in Iran. They hoped and prayed for release, not knowing when it would come or what demands would come with it. Throughout that time, Mona and those others clung to one thing, and this is why their story is told and retold. They clung to love—a seemingly superhuman love, and they held on to the very last. At the time, I hadn't heard of Mona, though I had learned, even living on the other side of the globe, something of the persecution of her community…

"A New Dress for Mona" is a play about the young Iranian martyr, Mona Mahmúdnizhád. Mona was a beautiful 16-year-old, full of life and promise, when, in 1983, she was executed, alongside nine other Bahá'í women, for no crime greater than teaching a children's class. Her remarkable faith and her supreme love were encapsulated in her final earthly act, when she kissed the hand of her executioner and the noose placed around her neck. To achieve such a station, however, Mona first had to triumph over fear and move past the natural anger towards injustice, and that journey is the focus of the play…

Love is at the heart of [this play], and the characters here are each, in some sense, suffused in love. There's the distant admiration of the young guard for Mona, and then there is Mona's awakening to a profound, consuming love to burn away all earthly appearances…

Here are lovers on their respective paths—some well-ahead and sprinting, some caught at a fork in the road, some dallying, and indeed some moving backwards. Each, in their way, offers an example to ponder. The phenomenon of drama permits us, as audience members, a kind of objectivity when we look at their situations that we often lack when looking at our own lives. Here we may sit and watch, defenses down, in a capacity similar to that of the seeker spoken of by Bahá'u'lláh in his great mystical work, *The Seven Valleys* :

> "*In this journey the seeker reacheth a stage wherein he seeth all created things wandering distracted in search of the Friend. How many a Jacob will he see, hunting after his Joseph; he will behold many a lover, hasting to seek the Beloved, he will witness a world of desiring ones searching after the One Desired.*"

The supreme example of love in Persian lore is Majnún, the insane one, who sifts through the dust in search of Laylí. Bahá'u'lláh recounts this ancient tale in *The Seven Valleys*, where we find Majnún steeped in the pain of long separation from his love, such that he cannot eat, he cannot sleep. Friends avoid him, and family cannot talk sense into him. He has let go of sense, for "*when the fire of love is ablaze, it burneth to ashes the harvest of reason.*" Majnún longs for death just to stop the pain. And so he sets out one night into the streets determined to end his life, and yet when confronted by the city's watchmen, he runs, fearful of the same. He runs and runs until he is cornered. And so, Majnún

> "*came to a garden wall, and with untold pain he scaled it, for it proved very high; and forgetting his life, he threw himself down to the garden. And there he beheld his beloved with a lamp in her hand, searching for a ring she had lost.*"

It seems it is not enough for the lover to tread the path of love, nor is it sufficient to sigh and pine. The lover must go to the wall. That is, the character of one's love must be proven, tested as gold in the fire, made evident in a climactic display. Majnun faced adversity and seeming injustice, personified by the watchmen, but he persevered and pushed on. He forgot himself and found his beloved. And as with Majnún, so too with the characters in [this play]: that which he feared, that which he ran from, turned out to be the means of his delivery.

In sharing this story, Bahá'u'lláh adopts and deepens the Sufi casting of the Majnún and Laylí story in a spiritual light, where Majnún is symbolic of the sincere, seeking soul and Laylí is the emblem of the Divine Beauty. Here then is an object-lesson not of the tragic turns of earthly love, but of that soul pure enough to attain the Divine Presence. This lover is an athlete in the spiritual arena, and the victory is the triumph over self. The opponents are the allied ranks of misbelief, of doubt, of apathy, of passivity, of distraction, of envy, of malice, of ambitiousness, and of fear. In this light, Majnún's lengthy period of separation tested the quality of his devotion. Such a one as holds any contradictory impulses is not yet ready, and if the so-called lover quickly moves on in pursuit of another, the superficiality of the love is revealed, torn up like a shallow-rooted weed. If, however, the lover is true, then such roots will only deepen with time, reaching out in all directions in search of the loved one. Love is, after all, manifest not only in lack of concentration and an inability to sleep. As is said in *The Hidden Words*, "*The sign of love is fortitude under My decree and patience under My trials.*" And when the time of real trial arrives, when the lover comes to the wall—partly impelled by internal need, partly compelled by outward circumstances, then that lover will need to dig down deep to muster the strength and the volition to mount that final obstacle, and then that soul may find itself, by the aid of the All-Merciful, delivered from the barren valley of remoteness to the blissful garden of reunion.

Here drama would appear the very able chronicler of the soul's test, for it cuts to the quick to find individuals in crisis, the lover at the wall. A recurring theme in so many stories is that the protagonists are called—as if from the plane of the spirit—to purify their moral characters, to so narrow and intensify their desires that only one choice remains, where there is no longer a dilemma, no longer a conflict for there is no way to return to the old ways once the crisis reaches its apex. Once at the wall, Majnún could only think to go up.

Not all characters will rise to the heights to which they are summoned, neither will all souls. Mona did, after her father did, after so many other martyrs… [The sacrifice of others is less absolute. We're all over the map, those] of us who are currently sheltered from the storms afflicting so much of humankind. We may think that, by avoiding war, famine, revolution and other external crises, we are free from being tested. But those who would count themselves among the lovers of God must, according to Bahá'u'lláh, awake and "*bestir ourselves*" to hear the cries of our fellow creatures and answer the urgent needs of our day.

There is a new standard of love in this Day. As part of humanity's awakening maturity, we are being called to a higher spiritual station, both individually and collectively. We are entering a period in which, Bahá'u'lláh says, the "*assayers of mankind* " will "*accept naught but purest virtue* " and when "*deeds done in the gloom of night* " will "*be laid bare and manifest before the peoples of the world.*" In this day, for example, steadfastness in one's faith is no longer the standard, but rather that joyous acceptance displayed in the face of grievous persecution by such heroes as Mona…

In the life cycle of humanity, this is a new age, an age of astonishing capacity, in which we are reaching for our social and spiritual maturation, the glorious birthright of our kind. We stand now collectively before a wall, the staggering height of which will require, if we will top it, everything we've got. This is the hardest climb we'll ever know, and yet what a garden of delight waits on the other side: the Kingdom on earth as it is in heaven, the realization of our essential unity.

MP
September 2011

Glossary

'Abdu'l-Bahá: eldest son of Bahá'u'lláh (1844–1921), the exemplar of the Bahá'í teachings, and the leader of the Faith from 1892 to 1921. (ab-DOL-ba-HA)

Alláh-u-abhá: Arabic for "God is most glorious," it is commonly used as a greeting among Bahá'ís. (al-LAH-o-ab-HA)

Alláh-u-akbar: Arabic for "God is most great," it is a common phrase used in the Islamic world. It is part of the call to prayer and a common chant in moments of zeal. (al-LAH-o-AK-bar)

Auxiliary Board Member: An appointed position in the Bahá'í administrative order. With no clergy, the Bahá'í community organizes its affairs through elected consultative bodies (*see* **Spiritual Assemblies**) and those they appoint to serve particular community needs.

Áyatu'lláh: a title referring to the most powerful priests within Shí'ih Islam. (AH-ya-TO-la)

Báb, The: the Prophet-Herald of the Bahá'í Faith (1819-1850). His revolutionary teachings resulted in brutal suppression by the Persian government and clergy. He foretold the coming of Bahá'u'lláh and was ultimately executed by firing squad. (bahb)

Bábí: a follower of the Báb. (bah-BEE)

Bahá'í: a follower of the Bahá'í Faith, a religion that originated in Iran in the mid-19th Century. While Bahá'ís have faced periods of intense persecution in Iran, the Faith has spread widely around the world and is now practiced by many millions of people from all different backgrounds. (Buh-HIGH)

Bahá'u'lláh: the Prophet-Founder of the Bahá'í Faith and its most important figure (1817-1892). His given name was Mírzá Husayn 'Alí; Bahá'u'lláh is a title that means "The Glory of God." He was from a noble Persian family, but was banished in 1852 at the height of persecutions against Bábís. A prisoner and exile for forty years, Bahá'u'lláh wrote voluminously, providing guidance and laying the foundations for what is now a world-wide religious community. (ba-HA-o-LA)

Chádor: a full-length body veil, almost like a tent, worn by some Iranian women in public. It is intended to cover all but the face. (cha-DOOR)

Imám: "leader" in Arabic. (e-MAHM)

Iran: a country in southwest Asia, formerly known as Persia. (ee-RAHN)

Islamic call to prayer: One of the religious practices of Islam is for people to assemble several times a day to pray. The call to prayer is delivered by an individual, the *muezzin*, whose chanting signals the people to gather.

Kabáb: the Persian version of barbecue, with prepared meat skewered and cooked over an open flame. Traditionally, men make the kabáb. (ka-BOB)

Mosque: an Islamic house of worship. (mosk)

Mullá: a title for a religious leader of the **Shí'ih** branch of Islam. (mol-LA)

Naw-Rúz: the Persian New Year, a festival which begins on the first day of Spring. It's a time of joyfulness, generosity and hospitality. The Bahá'í calendar also features the first day of Spring as its New Year. (no-ROOZ)

Persian: the predominant language of Iran. *Persia* is the old name for Iran, and the people are alternately called Iranians or Persians. In Persian, the language is called *fársí*. (PER-zhin)

Qur'án (also **Koran**)**:** the holy book of Islam. It is written in the Arabic language, and Muslims understand it to be the Word of God revealed through the Prophet Muhammad (570-632 C.E.). (kor-AHN)

Revolutionary Guard: a separate army raised up in Iran by the clergy during the Islamic Revolution of 1979. The Revolutionary Guard has been pivotal in establishing and maintaining the power of the clergy.

Riál: the official Iranian currency. In 1982, 1 Rial would be worth less than 5¢. (ree-AHL)

Ridván: An Arabic term for "Paradise," it is a 12-day festival beginning April 21 and is considered the holiest time of the Bahá'í calendar (RIZ-vahn)

Salaam: a greeting used in the Islamic world; Arabic for 'Peace.' (sa-LAHM)

Sháh: the King of Iran, often refers to Mohammad Reza Pahlavi, who lived 1919-1980 and ruled 1941-1979.

Shí'ih (also **Shiah, Shiite**): that branch of Islam predominant in Iran and some of the surrounding regions. (SHE-uh)

Shíráz: a major city in the south of Iran, famous for its roses and its poets, especially Hafez and Sa'di. (She-RAHZ)

Spiritual Assembly: the consultative body of 9 individuals elected annually in local Bahá'í communities. Spiritual Assemblies are also elected on a national level. Assembly members became targets of persecution during the Islamic Revolution, and as result, Bahá'í administration has been suspended in Iran since the 1980s.

Tumán: a unit of Iranian money, worth 10 Ríál. In 1982, a bail payment of 200,000 Tumán would be worth from US$50,000 to $75,000. (TOE-mahn)

Yá Bahá'u'l-abhá: Arabic for "O Glory of the Most Glorious," it is an invocation used by Bahá'ís in times of emergency, difficulty, elation, excitement, or other emotional extremity. (YA-ba-HA-ol-AB-ha)

Notes on History and Sources

There were four main written sources used in researching background for *A New Dress for Mona*: Olya's Story by Olya Roohizadegan; The Story of Mona: 1965-1983,* by the National Spiritual Assembly of Canada; "Mona's Life," a working title of an unpublished paper by an Iranian Bahá'í; and, most importantly, "Mona's Dream: Notes for a Film," an unpublished account by Farkhundih Mahmúdnizhád. The latter account is written as answers to questions posed by Mr. Alexei Berteig and translated by Ms. Gloria Shahzadeh.

1. "*Iran, Iran—Once the pearl of the world, exalted among nations.*" (I, i, 1)

   Iran is a Middle-Eastern country of nearly 80 million people, one of the largest and most influential countries in the region. The people of Iran, who overwhelmingly follow the Shí'ih branch of Islam, are ethnically quite distinct from their Arab neighbors to their west, who are mainly Sunni. The Persian language, while it has adopted the Arabic script and many Arabic words, is more closely related to Sanskrit or Latin. "Persian" is a word that is often used interchangeably with the term "Iranian." Despite its modern abasement, Iran's history is rich. Mona's references here are to Iran's contributions to some of the world's great religions—Zoroastrianism, Judaism, Christianity, and Islam.

2. "MONA *is now on the rug and plays a recording of herself chanting.*" (I, i, 1)

   Mona was highly creative from a young age and expressed herself through all manner of arts and crafts, including drawing, painting and collage. She had a lovely, soft voice, and would often tape record herself chanting prayers. Her mother has described Mona's propensity for visions, an aspect of her personality that the mother didn't understand. We might best ascribe this to a powerful intuition and imagination rather than some supernatural psychic power. The former is also more useful in dramatizing Mona's life, because it makes her more relatable, less iconic. In the play, we see what Mona sees and understand that it doesn't necessarily feel like

* See note in Introduction (p. ix) regarding Mona's age and birthdate.

a superpower, but perhaps even a handicap, as it makes concentrating on regular life difficult.

3. "*Ehsán Mehdízádeh. Sattár Khushkhú. Yadu'lláh Vahdat.*" (I, i, 1)

The three Bahá'í martyrs listed here were executed on the night of 30 April, 1981 in Shiraz by an ad-hoc firing squad. These men were prominent members of the Bahá'í community of Shiraz, and this event marked an uptick in the level of persecution in that important city. They were friends of the Mahmúdnizhád family, and so this tragic event hit close to home. As a maturing young Bahá'í, Mona was deeply stirred by the heroic sacrifice of these friends, just as she was troubled by the threat of heightening persecution. The execution scene that plays out here is based on an eyewitness account given in Olya's Story (pp 36-37). It includes the almost unthinkably dignified responses of Mr. Vahdat and of Ehsán, who was only 31 years old. This 1981 event took place before the play is set, but time and event are compressed for dramatic purposes.

4. "*Auxiliary Board Member!*" (I, i, 2)

Mr. Yadu'lláh Vahdat served for a number of years as an Auxiliary Board Member, an appointed position of significant responsibility in the Bahá'í community. The Iranian authorities first targeted those who played roles in national and local Bahá'í administration, thinking that if they cut off the head, so to speak, the body would die. As Bahá'ís in such positions were arrested and/or executed, other individuals would arise to serve in these roles. They then would be in danger themselves.

The most glaring and painful example of this involved the National Spiritual Assembly of Iran, that nationally-elected body of nine individuals who oversaw the affairs of Iran's largest religious minority. All nine members went missing in August 1980, never to be heard from again. A new national election raised nine more individuals, eight of whom would be captured and executed in December 1981. Soon thereafter, the National Spiritual Assembly was disbanded as an institution.

5. "EHSAN *kisses* ARAM*'s hand.*" (I, i, 2)

According to the eyewitness, Ehsán Mehdízádeh asked to have his blindfold removed, and he kissed the hand of the man assigned to shoot him. (Olya's Story, p. 37) Consistent with the Faith's abolition of the clergy, the Bahá'í teachings actually forbid the kissing of hands and the implied deference to the authority of religious and worldly leaders. Ehsán's action appears to breach this law in the letter, but not in the spirit. This is not an act of religious deference but of a kind of mystical appreciation and gratitude.

6. "*We thought the days of the martyrs had ended.*" (I, i, 3)

   The earliest days of the Bahá'í Faith—that is, during the 19th Century—were filled with persecution, with 20,000 martyrs targeted by fanatical clergy, mobs and government authorities. This extreme persecution had abated during much of the 20th century, but began to resume in the years of the Islamic Revolution.

7. "*My God, girl, what are you doing?*" (I, i, 3)

   Mona's mother, Farkhundih Anvarí Mahmúdnizhád, (1941?-2012) was from Abadan, Iran and had been born into a Bahá'í family. She married Yadu'lláh Mahmúdnizhád in 1958 in Qatar, and they later moved to Yemen. They had two daughters, Taráneh (b. 1961) and Mona (b. 1966). The family moved back to Iran around 1970 and had settled in Shíráz by 1973, when Mona was in 2nd grade. In her own words, "We made a heaven of Shiraz, a heaven of our dreams." The Mahmúdnizhád family lived in a modest flat on the 5th floor of an apartment building in the South of Shiraz. One of Mrs. Mahmúdnizhád's great gifts to posterity was her tireless efforts to tell the stories of her daughter and husband. Much of the detailed information in this play indeed comes from her account.

8. "*So talk to them about true Islam, not the regime…*" (I, i, 4)

   The Bahá'í Faith teaches the essential oneness of religion. Islam is regarded as a divine Revelation, the Qur'an a holy Book, and Muhammad a Messenger of God. There are obviously significant differences, however, in the interpretation of Islam and the Qur'an between the Bahá'í Faith and the fundamentalist doctrines widespread among the Shí'ih clergy in Iran.

9. "*The* FATHER *comes to her… He wipes her hand, caresses her hair.*" (I, i, 4)

   Mona's father, Yadu'lláh Mahmúdnizhád, was by all accounts a remarkable and saintly man. Born into a Shí'ih Muslim family in 1932, he lost his mother and father at an early age and was raised by an elderly uncle then by an older sister. He discovered the Bahá'í

Faith as a youth and engaged himself in its activities. He served the Bahá'í community of Shíráz in several capacities as teacher, administrator and leader, including acting as an Assistant to Mr. Vahdat. (See note 3.) He had worked at a Westinghouse factory repairing radios and TVs until the 1979 Revolution when he lost his job. He spent much of his time after the Revolution helping to educate the Bahá'í youth who had been expelled from university. As indicated here, he had a special relationship with Mona. According to Mrs. Madhmudnizhad, "when Mona grew older, this connection continued to grow" and "they could easily communicate by only looking at one another." Mrs. Mahmúdnizhád chose to call her husband Jamshíd, the Persian name his parents had given him, and not the Arabic name, Yadu'lláh, which his uncle had given him.

10. "*A school for girls. A* STUDENT *fervidly reads aloud her essay.*" (I, ii, 6)

Mona was respected and popular at school with both teachers and fellow students. She still attended school when most Bahá'í children had been expelled. Iran's public schools are now segregated along gender lines. This was especially important so soon after the Revolution, as so much emphasis was placed on returning women to traditional roles and removing them from spheres frequented by non-related men and where it was feared their chastity might be endangered.

11. "*You're not drawing flowers today.*" (I, ii, 6)

Like many young people, Mona loved nature and flowers and would often draw them or find other clever ways of making them. She was generally of good cheer, full of passion and excitement, and she loved to be with her friends. She deliberately worked to think positively and to overcome negative feelings. Still, the suffering of the Bahá'ís (and others) brought her great sadness. This combined with a strong sense of justice led her to speak out in ways that others might consider unsafe or unwise.

Farah is a composite character of fellow students and friends, including one friend named Tahmíneh. Farah is representative of many secular-minded Iranians. While Muslim, they are not fanatic and are more interested in practical day-to-day matters than in ideological considerations.

12. "*Our great leader, Ayatu'llah Khomeini, has brought us back from the dangerous path of westernization the Shah was pursuing.*" (I, ii, 7)

    The Iranian Revolution might well be seen, at least initially, as a popular response to the excesses of monarchy and westernization. Because of its rich oil resources, Iran became important to the West in the 20th Century. The countries of the West, especially Great Britain, and later the U.S., took a special interest and got involved in Iran's politics and economy. The Iranian Revolution began in the late 1970's when the clergy and other discontented elements ousted the *Sháh*, the King of Iran, from power. The clergy proved more powerful than other factions, and they set up an "Islamic Republic" where religious clerics dominated elected officials. *Áyatu'lláh Khomeini* was the principal leader of this Islamic Revolution. In February 1979, he returned from a long exile to become the supreme leader of the new government.

13. "*Freedom. Of all the great words in this great wide world…*" (I, ii, 7)

    Mona indeed wrote and presented such an essay on freedom responding to the prompt mentioned: '*The fruit of Islam is liberty and freedom of conscience, but you must taste it to understand.*' The final essay is lost, but an earlier draft exists and is reprinted in The Story of Mona. The essay dramatized here is based on that draft. This bold act got her in trouble, and she was sent to the principal. Her parents were called and they managed to keep her from being expelled. There is no direct evidence that this essay was particularly responsible for Mona being placed under surveillance. The simplified causal connections made here and in scenes that follow are for the sake of dramatization.

14. "*The Shí'ih Muslim cleric,* MULLA… *speaks, addressing a congregation.*" (I, iii, 9)

    In traditional Shí'ih Islam, the religious leaders—the 'ulamá (i.e., plural form of mullá)—have wielded extensive influence over their congregations. When strongman Rezá Pahlaví was Shah (1925-41), he pushed for secularization in Iran and weakened the authority of religious leaders. When his son, Mohammad Rezá, became king, the 'ulamá began to regain some of their strength and influence. With the Islamic Revolution, the religious leaders had power like never before. There were now no real secular leaders to moderate their influence.

The character of the Mulla here is a composite of religious clerics and prison officials, most notably Ayatu'lláh Qazá'í, the religious magistrate who sentenced Mona and the other 9 women to death.

15. "*How does it feel now, Muhammad Reza? Now you are king over a few cubic meters of foreign dirt?*" (I, iii, 9)

    The *Sháh*, Mohammed Rezá Pahlaví, had been King for nearly four decades. Now pressured from all sides to leave his country, he finally did so in January 1979. After a humiliating sequence of asylum seeking, he died of cancer an exile in 1980 and was buried in Cairo, Egypt.

16. "*Let us talk about a quiet corruption, let us talk about Bahá'í.*" (I, iii, 9)

    The Bahá'ís have been denounced by the Iranian clergy in a number of ways, ranging from direct charges of apostasy, or abandonment of the true Faith, to more far-fetched claims of espionage on behalf of Israel and the West. The Bahá'í community has been used as a political scapegoat for generations.

    Among the teachings of the Bahá'í Faith are that individuals should independently investigate the truth, that the clergy should be eliminated, and that men and women are equal and should be granted equal opportunity. It furthermore claims the appearance of a Messenger of God after Muhammad, namely, Bahá'u'lláh (1817-1892). These teachings set it in direct opposition to the Shí'ih orthodoxy, which considers Bahá'í a heretical sect. Despite this, the United Nations has acknowledged its independent status, and the Faith is well-established throughout the nations of the world with members representing every kind of racial and religious background.

17. "*This is why we make hijab universally applicable.*" (I, iii, 9)

    Hijáb most often denotes the traditional head-covering worn by women in the Muslim world. Before the Revolution of 1979, Iran had become quite westernized in its dress and entertainments. The Islamic Revolution quickly made laws of more traditional practices, such as women covering up their hair in public. These laws came to be enforced somewhat more gradually. Act I of the play shows that gradual reintroduction through dramatic compression so that by the time of the arrest, it is mandatory. In Iran, it is considered most important to cover the hair but the face can show.

18. "*otherwise those lips… could give a horn to a holy man.*" (I, iii, 10)

    The implication here is that this Mulla is rather lustful. Of course, religious leaders in Islam are not bound by the same celibacy practices as those in, say, Roman Catholicism. They often have several wives, and some practices allow religious cover for one-night stands! Concerning the political erosion of women's rights in Iran, it doesn't take much of a psychologist to understand that fanatics so focused on controlling women's sexuality and perceived threats to their chastity may well be projecting their own concupiscence on the society in general. Giving this element of sexuality to the character seemed important therefore, though not as essential as giving him a ruthless intelligence. Neither is an inherent characteristic to the office for any individual, but in a representative of the 'ulamá collectively, these feel spot on.

19. "*Your eminence, you remember my cousin, Aram?*" (I, iii, 10)

    Árám is also a composite character, though a more complicated one than Farah or the Mulla. First, he represents that young Iranian male coming of age in a time of war when military service is mandatory. As he later says, he chose to join the Revolutionary Guard in order to avoid going to the war in Iraq, an atrocious eight-year debacle with casualties of up to a million Iranians and half-a-million Iraqis. Árám carries no ill-will and seems more interested in love than politics. Second, he has that vein of poetry within him emblematic of Iran's highest cultural attainments, but now subjugated to the brutal and arbitrary rule of the clerics' ignorance and dogma. The consequent pall of shame that covers such people of good-will who have been coerced to do evil in times of violent social upheaval is seen in his haunting by the phantom of Ehsan. Furthermore, Árám is used by the play as a kind of divine teaching tool for Mona. He becomes the flashpoint for many of her emotional turns, from puzzlement, to borderline-romantic sentiment, to deep fear, then rage and hatred, and finally forgiveness. In this one character live the actions of dozens of actual people, including Ehsán Mehdízádeh's executioner, the guard who followed/spied on Mona, one of the arresting guards, several of the prison guards, and finally Mona's executioner. All of them can be contained in one dramatic character, because, at best, they each had a motivation where self-preservation trumped conscience. That is the hallmark of Arám. Incidentally, the name Árám in Persian means "calm" or "stillness."

As for Guards 1 and 2, they stand in for all those Revolutionary Guards and prison guards encountered by our central characters. In Iranian society, the Revolutionary Guard are often thought to be taken from the most fanatical and uneducated segments of society. Guard 1 is a bit more sympathetic and is a cousin to Arám. Guard 2 is the more fanatical and he takes on the role of a prison interrogator. It is purposeful that Guard 2 is the one who torments Mr. Mahmúdnizhád and then later helps him walk. This is a dramatic testament to the true transformative effect the Bahá'í prisoners have had on their captors.

20. "*What happened at the cemetery today?… People get emotional sometimes.*" (I, iii, 10)

    The martyrdom of these three Bahá'ís was a critical moment in the collective suffering of the Shiraz Bahá'í community. Word spread rapidly about the execution when the bodies of these three martyrs were delivered to the Bahá'í cemetery. A huge crowd of mourners, Bahá'í and some Muslim, came out to pay their respects. They were not admitted to the cemetery by the guards who had been posted there by the authorities. The guards were demanding people leave, but nobody moved and all remained gathered in front of the gate. Eventually, word was sent that the Local Spiritual Assembly was asking the friends to disperse, and they immediately did. A large memorial gathering was held there some days later.

21. "EHSAN, *the martyr from Scene 1, has entered, now as an apparition.*" (I, iii, 10)

    The Bahá'í Faith does not concern itself much with the idea of ghosts. While it does not flatly deny supernatural occurrences in the physical realm, it downplays their relevance and influence in our lives. Here though, the apparition of Ehsán is intended as an external manifestation of Arám's shame and the recurring memory of his participation in a grave injustice. In other words, this is not intended to literally be Ehsán's ghost. We may assume Ehsán's spirit is flying high in the Abhá Kingdom (i.e., heaven).

22. "*I couldn't tell Bahá'ís from Muslims.*" (I, iii, 11)

    Unlike members of some other minority religions in the region, the Bahá'ís do not represent a distinct ethnic group. Many Baha'is originally came from the Persian lineage and the Shí'ih religion the majority of Iran hails from, while others came from its minority tribes and religions, including the Zoroastrians, Jews and Christians.

23. "*A poet? So, Hafez, let's hear one.*" (I, iii, 11)

    Háfez is a 14th Century poet who came from Shiraz, known as the city of poets and roses. Hafez is considered the National Poet of Iran, and everyday Iranians memorize and recite his poems and sayings. A volume of his poetry is traditionally used in Persian households for fortune-telling or advice-seeking, a divination manual like the I-Ching in China. The Tomb of Hafez in Shiraz, with its beautiful gardens and memorials, is a great attraction for the city's inhabitants and for visitors and tourists.

24. "*Go bring me my rug. It's time for prayer.*" (I, iii, 12)

    Muslims are obligated to pray 5 times a day. Throughout the Muslim world, the call to prayer rings out from mosques at the appointed times. There is some difference between Sunni and Shí'ih observance of obligatory prayer in gesture and language, but the fundamentals are the same. A small prayer rug is often used by believers in performing their prayers.

25. "*Yes, some of the Bahá'ís seem to embody remarkable virtue…*" (I, iii, 12)

    In Iran, among the fair-minded populace, the Bahá'ís have long had a reputation for being honest, forgiving and forbearing. They have borne so much adversity for so long without turning to revenge or violence that many of their fellow citizens are now, in the second decade of the 21st Century, arising to champion their innocence. This includes prominent lawyers, activists, scholars, thinkers and artists. This was not the case in the early 1980s when the religious leaders held more clout and their pronouncements carried more weight, when the followers were misled and the rest were silent.

26. "*What would people say if they saw that the Revolutionary Guard had such soft hands?*" (I, iii, 12)

    The *Revolutionary Guard* is an independent army first raised up by the powerful Shí'ih clergy during the Islamic Revolution of the late 1970's. This Guard, separate from the regular army, enforced the will of the clergy, and were directly responsible for much of the persecution of Bahá'ís. Since the beginning of the Revolution, the

Revolutionary Guard has gained enormous power and wealth. In 2009, they upheld their reputation for brutality in violently suppressing the Green Movement, a broad-based peaceful political uprising.

27. "…*the* MOTHER *with a dark chador…*" (I, iv, 13)

    As described in the glossary, a chádor is "a dark, full-length body veil, almost like a tent, worn by some Iranian women in public" and "intended to cover all but the face." It is not form-fitting or sewn together, but wrapped over the hijáb head covering like the hood of a cape. When walking in public, women would often need one hand just to hold the chádor in place, clasping the fabric just underneath the chin.

28. "*You're one of the few Bahá'í children still in school… It's not like I can go to university anyway.*" (I, iv, 13)

    At the height of the Revolution, all schools were shut down for the remainder of the school year. When they reopened, there were new rules. While Bahá'í students had always been subject to discrimination and derision in the classroom, now they were subject to increased scrutiny and oftentimes expulsion. This is at the elementary and secondary levels. At the University level, Bahá'í students were simply expelled and professors fired. On all admissions forms, there is a question about the applicant's religion, and Bahá'ís are prohibited from attending. (And in their Faith, they are not permitted to dissemble their religion for the sake of expediency.) In the immediate wake of these expulsions, individuals such as Mona's father arose to educate the youth. Then in 1987, an underground, informal network called the Bahá'í Institute for Higher Education was started by many of those same educators. It soon grew and it continues to this day, despite harassment, vandalism of its properties, and arrest and imprisonment of its faculty, administration and staff.

29. "*In one hundred forty years, when have the people of this country ever stood up for us?*" (I, iv, 13)

    As indicated in the preceding notes, Iran's religious and political authorities have ruled with threat and manipulation such that the rights of the country's largest religious minority (i.e., the Bahá'ís) could be constantly assailed with no popular backlash. There is some sense that this is beginning to change now, thirty-odd years after Mona's death, and that some courageous, fair-minded individuals are speaking out on behalf of the Baha'is. Still those voices are far outnumbered by those who are silent.

30. "*...this is Iran, the land of Cyrus the Great, the founder of human rights!*" (I, iv, 13)

    Iran has had a rich past with distinguished ages of influence and civilization. The first golden age was the time of the Achaemenid kings of the 6th and 5th Centuries B.C., who included Cyrus the Great, Darius, Xerxes and Artaxerxes. These kings are generally praised in the Bible for their justice and for supporting the Jews in their efforts to repopulate the Holy Land and rebuild their Temple in Jerusalem after the Babylonian conquest. The idea of Cyrus as the founder of human rights refers to a famous pronouncement of the king's tolerant and peaceful intentions upon conquering and entering Babylon. This is recorded on a clay cylinder called the Cyrus cylinder.

31. "*It's Mona's sister,* TARANEH, *21 and pregnant.*" (I, iv, 14)

    Taráneh Mahmúdnizhád is Mona's older sister by five years. By this point, Taráneh had married and moved out of the family home. She gave birth to her first child, Nura, in January 1982. Mona adored babies and children including her niece. Taráneh, like her mother, has worked to keep alive the memory of her sister and father.

32. "*Bahá'u'lláh says we're like the baby in the womb and the spiritual world is all around us.*" (I, iv, 14)

    Cf., "The world beyond is as different from this world as this world is different from that of the child while still in the womb of its mother. When the soul attaineth the Presence of God, it will assume the form that best befitteth its immortality and is worthy of its celestial habitation." (Bahá'u'lláh, Gleanings from the Writings of Bahá'u'lláh, p. 157.)

33. "MONA *sees a beautiful* WOMAN IN WHITE." (I, iv, 15)

    The Woman in White is a composite character as well, representing the various conveyers of divine confirmation that Mona experienced. The clearest human being we might associate her with is the great Bábí poet, feminist, scholar and heroine, Tahirih, who was martyred herself in 1852, famously wearing a bridal dress for the occasion. Several of Mona's dreams and visions included the Prophet-Founder of the Bahá'í Faith, Bahá'u'lláh, or His Son and Successor, 'Abdu'l-Bahá. Bahá'ís choose not to dramatically represent these souls out of respect, so the Woman in White stands in for them as well. Notes will indicate the actual story behind such interactions. This appearance in scene 4 is invented.

34. "*I don't know that we shouldn't get out of Iran altogether at least until this whole thing blows over.*" (I, iv, 15)

    The rise in persecutions did cause many Iranian Bahá'ís to consider their options. Some moved elsewhere in the country, especially to rural areas, where there was less risk. Some paid smugglers high prices to be taken at considerable risk across the border to Turkey or Pakistan, where they would then seek asylum in North America, Europe or Australia. Others felt they should not abandon their native homes despite the risk. The Mahmúdnizhád family had tried several years prior to move to one of the Arab nations. Their opportunity to do this fell through and Mr. Mahmúdnizhád took it as a sign they needed to stay in Shiraz. Like the Mahmúdnizhád family, the majority of Iranian Baha'is stayed put.

35. "*...she's going to this orphanage three times a week now, these tiny neglected kids call her 'Mommy Mona'...*" (I, iv, 16)

    When Mona was 13 years old, her teacher took her class to an orphanage. Mona was so moved by the children and their wretched condition that she began to volunteer there. At first, Mona was secretive about going, fearing that her mother would not let her go. Once caught, she told her mother about the first time she went: "One of the kids came forward and asked me if I would like to be her mother. Without thinking, I sat and took her little hand in mine, kissed her beautiful face and told her that I would love to have a lovely daughter like her. A few days later, I felt that the little girl was expecting me, so I went to see her at the orphanage, but I found her sick in bed. Her beautiful eyes were swollen and red. As soon as she saw me, she said, 'mom, you came!' Then the other children came round me and asked for my name. I told them that I was their mother."

    Mona then described the filthy conditions and that "the children cried together in such a way that even a heart of stone could be moved to tears. It was then that I decided to do my best to help these children, so I asked the person in charge to allow me to go there a couple of times a week to bathe the children… [N]ow when I go there, as soon as the children see me they call out and say 'Mommy Mona is here.' " Mona would bring them biscuits, cheese puffs, storybooks and crayons. She continued, "I sit down in the middle, while they hover over me by caressing my hair or sitting on my lap, and they show me the sort of affection that every child would like to show his mother. In this way, I can somewhat provide for them something which would in some way make up for not having a mother. Mother, there is no pleasure greater than this! I clean the smaller children; I bathe them; I put them in diapers; and if there is any time left, I take them in my arm and give them milk from a bottle. They then put their arms around me and touch my eyes and ears with their little fingers and go to sleep with a smile on their lips. In this way, I do what I can for them and consider myself the most fortunate mother in the world." ("Notes for a Film," Farkhundih Mahmúdnizhád)

Mona's family was not wealthy. She would pay for the snacks and supplies with her small allowance and by saving her taxi fare and making the long walk to and from school. She also worked in a market in the summer. Mona continued to visit the orphanage for three years until the time she was arrested. In prison, Mona told her mother she missed the children terribly.

36. "MRS. KHUDAYAR, *a neighbor, enters.*" (I, iv, 16)

Mrs Khudáyár is based on the family's Muslim neighbor, Mrs. Gazvaní, though the characterization is fictional. Mrs. Gazvaní had daughters that were friends with Mona, so Reza is fictional. Then again there is always an awkward boy around falling in love with a lovely girl like Mona.

37. "*I have something for you. A gift. But you must choose.*" (I, v, 18)

The dream of the three dresses is basically historical, though dramatized here. I heard Olya Roohizadegan, a fellow prisoner, speak of this dream in October 1994 in St. Petersburg, Florida as she was touring around the United States. It was from this account that I first developed the play. Much later I learned that Mona was not offered dresses but something more like capes, with a clasp at the neck. And yet we have a play made out of dresses, and with that I am content. Another important difference was that Mona didn't actually say "no" to the first two offers, though it seems she made diplomatic if unenthusiastic replies. Such indirectness is common in Persian culture. Here is Mrs. Mahmúdnizhád's brief account:

"She had had a vision of Bahá'u'lláh in which He had given her three capes. The first cape was a red one. While giving her the red cape, Bahá'u'lláh had told her that it was the cape of martyrdom and had asked if she accepted it in His path? Mona had responded, 'I do, if it be Your will; if it be Your desire!' He had then given her a black cape saying that it was the cape of sorrow and adversity and again asking her if she would accept it in His path? And she had responded, 'how beautiful are the tears that are shed in Your path.' The third cape was a blue one, which Bahá'u'lláh had placed over Mona's shoulders and closes the button with His own Hands and said, 'This is the cape of service in My path.' "

38. "ARAM *has remained in the same place, as if he's still in Mona's sight.*" (I, v, 19)

The dream left a profound impression on Mona, which she identified viscerally with feeling Bahá'u'lláh's fingers fasten a button of the blue cape against her chest. The inclusion of the young man in the dream is fictional. It plants the question for Mona and audience, who is this young man and what destiny connects them? That is finally answered by the end of the play, but Mona fashions many guesses along the way.

39. "*How did that tape get in there? That music's unclean!*" (I, vi, 22)

Unclean (Persian: "najes") is a concept that certain people, animals or things are inherently impure and/or that association with them causes believers to enter a state of religious impurity (i.e., that without a ritualized purification, their prayers will be unacceptable to God.). Western-influenced (or other non-religious) music is an example of something that might be unclean as interpreted by certain religious leaders. According to the Shí'ih clergy in Iran, Bahá'ís are unclean, as is brought up in a later scene.

40. "ARAM… *stares at* MONA. *He wears nothing that might distinguish him as a guard.*" (I, vi, 22)

As mentioned earlier (Note 19), Mona did have a guard following her. She told her mother one day that a man had been following her wherever she went. At first, she thought he might have just been going to the same place or places. Her mother told her to be careful, but Mona said then she wouldn't be able to carry out her service of visiting people, encouraging them, sharing news and teaching children. She decided to think of him as a brother protecting her. Boys didn't harass her on the street with him there. She said, "I feel bad that he has to wait on the street for hours for me to finish my business in a home and return. Sometimes, I even let him know from afar before I go in that I may take a couple of hours or more." Later they realized he was from the Revolutionary Guard and was making a list of everything she did and everywhere she went.

41. "*They stopped calling us Bábís a hundred years ago.*" (I, vi, 23)

 Bábís were followers of the Báb, the Prophet-Herald of the Bahá'í Faith, who announced His mission in 1844. The generality of the Bábí community became Bahá'ís after Bahá'u'lláh in 1863 declared Himself as the fulfillment of the Báb's promises. After that, the Bábí title was replaced by Bahá'í, which simply means 'follower of Bahá (Glory)'. Still, the term Bábí might be used as an epithet by the ignorant or the malicious. There is a great amount of prejudice and misinformation circulated among the Iranian populace about the Bahá'ís.

42. "*There is tension in the air, as if he's delivered news she did not want to hear.*" (I, vii, 24)

 Mrs. Mahmúdnizhád said, "As for the matter of his [Mr. Mahmúdnizhád's] appointment as a member of the Auxiliary Board, I knew that this would guarantee his arrest, because he was also the secretary of the LSA [Local Spiritual Assembly] of Shiraz. I was worried that his workload would increase and that he would have to work night and day, which would endanger his health. Of course his appointment as an ABM [Auxiliary Board Member] put his life more at risk as well."

43. "*This place needs to be cleaned. I'm going shopping. I'm writing a list for you.*" (I, vii, 24)

 According to her mother, Mona "attended to all the housework. I used to work as a seamstress [at home] and had no time for the housework; therefore, Mona did everything, from housecleaning to laundry, to cooking and baking." From reading the accounts, one can surmise that Mrs. Mahmúdnizhád suffered with ill-health and also some depression and anxiety. This is not a surprising response given the extreme circumstances in which they were living. Her husband and daughter both worked hard to ease her burden.

44. "*The* FATHER *winces some and holds his stomach.*" (I, vii, 25)

Mr. Mahmúdnizhád had a stomach ulcer that went back to times of trouble and deprivation when they lived in Yemen in the 1960s. He used to drink warm milk to soothe it. Stomach ulcers of course get worse with stress.

45. "*The boy who's following you. It's been days now I've seen him.*" (I, vii, 26)

In Iranian cities, there is a cultural pattern of boys following girls in the streets. It's not considered so serious as "stalking," and it's not assumed that the boy has bad intent. Protective male members of the girl's family may well threaten him or chase him off though.

46. "*It arrived unsealed—those goons with the Revolutionary Guard can't admit they're censoring the mail.*" (I, vii, 27)

The Iranian authorities used and continue to use such means as phone-tapping and mail censoring in their attempt to gather information on the Bahá'ís.

47. "*I have been told that your tea—Bahá'í tea—is a potion that brainwashes people to become Bahá'ís.*" (I, vii, 27)

One rather humorous example of the widespread misinformation about Bahá'ís is the belief that if you drink their tea, you will be brainwashed into becoming a Bahá'í yourself. In a culture where sharing tea is an essential aspect of hospitality, one can see how this superstition serves to keep Muslims from socializing with Bahá'ís.

48. "*They want me to teach a Bahá'í children's class.*" (I, vii, 28)

Fifteen is considered the age of maturity in the Bahá'í Faith. When Mona turned fifteen, she officially registered as a Bahá'í and also applied to be part of a children's education committee. She began teaching children's classes at this point. Taking after her father, she poured her energy into her service, even to the point of overextending herself and struggling to get her homework done. One of the official criminal charges against Mona was that she taught a Bahá'í children's class. The Bahá'í community probably would not have communicated this request in letter form given the risk, but dramatizing it as such helps us understand their constant sense of being watched and needing to be vigilant.

49. "*Just leave me your books—Taraneh wants them too, but I'll use them more.*" (I, vii, 28)

    Strange as it seems, Mona and Taráneh were so certain their father would go to prison and even be executed, that they used to squabble over who would get his library of Bahá'í books when he was gone.

50. "*It's a new dress for Mona. And a new Mona must step into it.*" (I, vii, 29)

    The delivery of the dress is completely fictional and used for dramatic purposes. This moment in the play signals a kind of break, and it ends on a positive and hopeful note. In a three-act structure, this would be the end of Act I. In our UNC production, the company came out and did a choreographed Persian dance they had learned.

51. "*Yes.* (*Sees* ARAM *waiting for her.*) *Hello.*" (I, viii, 31)

    In Iranian society, boys and girls who do not know each other do not generally interact. There is little of the ready familiarity with strangers of the opposite sex that you can find in the West. This action of Mona's is fictional. It's not unthinkable, but would have seemed rather forward.

52. "*Once upon a time, there was a lover named Majnun…*" (I, ix, 32)

    The story of Laylí and Majnún is an ancient story based on an Arab legend and most famously told by Nizami, the 12th century Persian poet. Bahá'u'lláh recounts a version of the story in the mystical work, *The Seven Valleys,* and this is the version that Mona paraphrases here. See "The Lover at the Wall" excerpt, pp. 85-88, for a related discussion of the story.

    As mentioned above (Note 48), Mona became a Bahá'í children's class teacher, following the model of her father, who worked with youth and young adults.

53. "*So who wants some cheese puffs?*" (I, ix, 33)

    It's a sweet little detail. As with the kids in the orphanage, Mona used to treat the students in her children's class to snacks such as cheese puffs, which she bought with the money she would save by sacrificing her own pleasure.

54. "MONA *sneaks up on him and grabs the notebook, startling him.*" (I, x, 36)

This is fictional. Such a direct confrontation with the guard following her would have been very unlikely, especially given Iranian norms. At some point though, Mona would have realized and processed the threat not just to her father but to herself. The calmness with which she told her mother the story (See Note 40) may have been, at least partially, a product of Mona not wanting to worry her mother.

55. "*My dear, someone's been following me for years.*" (I, xi, 37)

    Mr. Mahmúdnizhád was among the most prominent and loved Bahá'ís in Shiraz. He was long the subject of surveillance, and everyone expected him to be arrested.

56. "*So who would take care of those who can't leave?*" (I, xi, 38)

    As terribly as the Bahá'ís have been treated, so many stand out as true patriots who dedicate themselves to the good of their community. While thousands did decide to leave, the majority of the Iranian Baha'is did remain in their native land. They have persisted in the face of decades of systematic oppression that has all but extinguished hope for any sort of normal life.

57. "*What does Bahá'u'lláh say, 'I have made death a messenger of joy to thee. Wherefore dost thou grieve?'*" (I, xi, 38)

    The Writings of Bahá'u'lláh both exalt the station of martyrdom and counsel Bahá'ís to behave with wisdom so as to avoid persecution. Life on this earthly plane and the opportunity to serve it offers are gifts. At the same time, death is nothing to fear, but a birthing into a new and greater spiritual reality. The entire passage referred to here: "O SON OF THE SUPREME! I have made death a messenger of joy to thee. Wherefore dost thou grieve? I made the light to shed on thee its splendor. Why dost thou veil thyself therefrom?" (The Hidden Words, Arabic, #32)

58. "*Then you will be a true Bahá'í.*" (I, xi, 39)

    There is a beautiful passage from a talk 'Abdu'l-Bahá gave in New York in 1912 as He was preparing to return to the Holy Land. In it, He sums up the core Bahá'í teachings, and I include an extended excerpt because of its direct relevance to Mona's journey:

    "You must manifest complete love and affection toward all mankind. Do not exalt yourselves above others, but consider all as your equals, recognizing them as the servants of one God. Know that God is compassionate toward all; therefore, love all from the depths of your hearts, prefer all religionists before yourselves, be filled with love for every race, and be kind toward the people of all nationalities. Never speak disparagingly of others, but praise without distinction. Pollute not your tongues by speaking evil of another. Recognize your enemies as friends, and consider those who wish you evil as the wishers of good. You must not see evil as evil and then compromise with your opinion, for to treat in a smooth, kindly way one whom you consider evil or an enemy is hypocrisy, and this is not worthy or allowable. You must consider your enemies as your friends, look upon your evil-wishers as your well-wishers and treat them accordingly. Act in such a way that your heart may be free from hatred. Let not your heart be offended with anyone. If someone commits an error and wrong toward you, you must instantly forgive him... Be illumined, be spiritual, be divine, be glorious, be quickened of God, be a Bahá'í." ('Abdu'l-Bahá, The Promulgation of Universal Peace, p. 452-453)

59. "*This is the House of the Báb. This is where my Faith began.*" (I, xii, 40)

The House of the Báb is revered by Bahá'ís, the spot where on 22 May 1844, Siyyid 'Alí Muhammad, known as the Báb (or "the Gate"), declared His divine mission to His first follower, the event signaling the birth of a new world religion, the Bahá'í Faith. In its history and during the Revolution, the House of the Báb was several times vandalized. In the summer of 1979, officials confiscated the property, and demolition work was several times attempted, but then quickly suspended due to freak accidents, such as one where a man died when a wall fell on him. The House was finally demolished in the dead of night in December of the same year. (See Olya's Story, pp. 20-27)

60. "*So, in the front here was a wall about this tall…*" (I, xii, 40)

The street leading to the House was more like an alley, and the style of the house wouldn't permit one to look into the yard. Rather the outside had a high wall, and walking in, one entered the courtyard where an orange tree (planted by the Báb) would have been located. There is a mosque nearby, from which people can monitor, even today, those who come to visit that spot. The site was eventually made into a parking lot.

Mona did make a pilgrimage to the ruins of the House of the Báb, and it had a profound effect on her. In the play it seems like the same night as the arrest, but this is just dramatic compression.

61. "*They're down there now begging him to go into hiding. There are rumors of arrests.*" (I, xiii, 42)

    Mrs. Mahmúdnizhád said, "The [Bahá'í] youth in Shiraz loved Mr. Mahmúdnizhád very much. A few days prior to the arrest [of Mr. Mahmúdnizhád], some of the youth came to our home and begged him to leave Shiraz, inasmuch as they feared that his arrest was inevitable. However, Mr. Mahmúdnizhád told them that he was a soldier of the Blessed Beauty and that he would not leave his post. They offered to come and place a peephole on our door, so that whenever the revolutionary guards came to take him, we would know by looking through it and would not open the door. In order not to hurt the youth, Mr. Mahmúdnizhád agreed to their suggestion, so they came and installed the peephole and went."

62. "*What if I took your rug and some other things…*" (I, xiii, 42)

    Indeed the neighbors, Mrs. Gazvaní and her husband, did offer to take their belongings including their furniture, carpets, clothing and books. Mrs. Mahmúdnizhád recounted, "When I saw that they meant well, I accepted their offer." When Mr. Mahmúdnizhád returned and noticed items missing, he requested everything be brought back, saying "Do you want me to be ashamed for not having anything to give in the path of the Blessed Beauty? Do you want me to sacrifice my home empty of its carpets?"

    Personally I love how these two last examples—the peephole and the carpets—might seem in Mrs. Mahmúdnizhád's mind to involve the same principle of acceding to the wishes of those who intend well. Her husband, however, saw a very distinct spiritual principle in the latter. This account makes me admire him yet empathize with her.

63. "*Why did I have to hear that the girl and her friend were walking on that damned spot by someone else?*" (I, xiv, 44)

    This interaction is fictional. We have no information on conversations among the Revolutionary Guard or details about surveillance.

64. "*They don't usually target women, much less girls like me.*" (I, xv, 45)

Up until this point in Shiraz, mostly Bahá'í men had been imprisoned and only men had been executed. Elsewhere in Iran, however, Bahá'í women had been executed, and in Shiraz, women had been injured and killed in mob violence.

65. "*See that bright star near the moon. Look at it and I'm right there with you.*" (I, xv, 45)

    This little exchange is true and happened between Mona and her friend Tahmíneh.

66. "*You think I care about the rug?... Let's say, just hypothetically, that Reza here...*" (I, xvi, 46)

    See Note 62.

67. "*When I finish school this year, maybe we can look at colleges in other places. We can go to Africa, or America.*" (I, xvi, 47-48)

    While Mona had strong premonitions of her martyrdom, this is not to say that she had no ambitions or interest in the world. According to her mother, she loved traveling and historical sites. She talked to her mother about going to remote villages with a back-pack and bare-feet, also traveling to the Amazon, Africa and India.

68. "*...we used to move so often, and every time you would go ahead and prepare the house...*" (I, xvi, 48)

    Mrs. Mahmúdnizhád said, "Our lifestyle dictated us to move around all the time. Whenever, we were about to go to a new city, we spent a few days in the home of a friend or relative until Mr. Mahmúdnizhád found a place for us in the new town. He usually arranged the furniture and then came to invite us to our new home. However, we never spent much time apart; we were separated for a few days or a week, at a time, at the most." This story would of course have a beautiful and sadly ironic twist that is referred to in Act 2, Scene 6.

69. "*Revolutionary Guard, open up!*" (I, xvi, 48)

    According to Mrs. Mahmúdnizhád, on the night of the arrest, "we hosted a gathering for Mr. Mahmúdnizhád's assistants who had come from in and around Shiraz to consult with him in his capacity as a member of the Auxiliary Board. Mona was wearing a green blouse and a green and cream checkered skirt, and looked particularly handsome with her green eyes and straight long hair.

She spent all day serving the guests, and, once they had left, she started to study for her English exam, which was scheduled for the next day. Mr. Mahmúdnizhád said that he would help himself to some dinner, and I went to take a bath because I was exhausted. I had just came out of the bathroom and was still wearing a towel on my head when I heard a violent knock on the door." The arrest scene as portrayed here is based on Mrs. Mahmúdnizhád's account, the version Mona told Olya Roohizadegan recorded in Olya's Story, and the research of another Iranian Bahá'í. Except for the business with Árám and Mrs. Khudáyár, it keeps quite close to the original. The original search though took much longer. The guards entered at 9pm and stayed about three hours.

70. "*They're not home. Why don't you come back later?*" (I, xvi, 48)

    The Muslim neighbors across the hall tried to intercede and tell the Guards the family was not home.

71. "*You are not my father and you're not my brother, so I have to cover my hair in your presence.*" (I, xvi, 49)

    Normally when the guards entered one's home, they asked the women to wear Islamic attire. In this case, they didn't, but Mona insisted with the above statement despite them ordering her to sit down. She went to her room and put on a headscarf. Coming out, Mona tried again to study her English, fully expecting that only her father would be taken. She clearly showed anger and disdain for the guards. The implication of her line "you're not my brother" is so beautifully juxtaposed with the father's line "I love these brothers like my own sons." That is the central conflict of the play in miniature. Before leaving, Mona managed to hide some documents that would have endangered some Bahá'í friends if discovered. Incidentally, the detail about Mona being in the bathroom when the guards knocked on the door is also apparently accurate.

72. "*Sure, but maybe while you're searching, I can take them too.*" (I, xvi, 50)

    This is fictional, though quite plausible. One guard remained in the hallway and warned all the neighbors to remain in their homes until midnight.

73. "*They are unclean.*" (I, xvi, 50)

    See Note 39.

74. "*You, you want your son to go fight in Iraq?*" (I, xvi, 50)

The Iran-Iraq war is mentioned above (Note 19). In 1982, Iran was in the midst of a terrible and costly war with Iraq. Among other brutalities of war, Saddam Hussein's army used chemical weapons against the Iranian soldiers.

75. "*Jamshid, they're going to take you.*" (I, xvi, 50)

    This line and some of the other dialogue between the Mother and the Guards is taken from the historical account. They were all surprised that Mona was being taken. The guard's statement about Mona's writing and her tapes is telling. They feared her fearless and eloquent power of expression.

76. "*These men. I love these brothers like my own sons. I am sure it is the will of God…*" (I, xvi, 51)

    This amazing short monologue is recorded in Olya's Story, this account apparently shared by Mona. It's not word-for-word the way Mrs. Mahmúdnizhád recalls it, though the focus on submission to the Will of God is the same. In addition to his universal and accepting vision, notice there is an element of protection he's seeking by calling on the young men's higher selves that they will not hurt his daughter.

77. "*Mom, it won't be a prison for me, but an open field, a mountain top where I can touch the moon. Please don't worry. We'll see you soon.*" (I, xvi, 52)

    This is a paraphrase of the words Mona reportedly said as she left her mother. The night was 23 October, 1982, and about 40 Bahá'ís, including 6 women, were arrested and imprisoned in a single sweep. Mona was the first Bahá'í woman to arrive at the 'Sepah' jail that night. She was given two thin, dirty blankets and she laid down to sleep, but soon other Bahá'í women began to arrive. All were shocked to find young Mona there. After about a month in the Sepah jail, she and others were moved to Adelabad prison. More arrests came and more Bahá'í prisoners arrived that fall, as anti-Bahá'í persecution in Shiraz was nearing its peak.

78. "MONA *stands blindfolded. She is refusing to answer questions…*" (II, i, 53)

    The interrogations that the prisoners faced were severe. They went on day after day, lasting all day and into the early morning. The authorities used various methods, including torture, to get confessions of crimes, names and activities of other Bahá'ís, and the grand prize—the recanting of one's Bahá'í belief. Standing for hours, blindfolds, sleep deprivation and verbal abuse were the minimum. Mona may well have faced torture, but she never shared it with her mother. Mona and the other prisoners had all agreed to meet their interrogators with silence. They had not committed any crimes after all.

79. "*I put my trust in God to get this letter to you—and in Mínú who is smuggling it out…*" (II, i, 53)

    Mona surprisingly managed to send out a couple of letters while in prison. The letter Farah reads here is not an actual one from Mona, but its contents are factual. The Mínú referred to is Mínú Anvari, a young Bahá'í woman who was released. The image of Mona herself on a balcony getting closer to the moon but seeing her mother's face comes from Mona's words recorded in Olya's Story.

80. "*Look, I know this is more your parents' religion than yours.*" (II, i, 54)

    This might have been a particular provocation for Mona. A central tenet in the Bahá'í Faith is the independent investigation of truth, and Mona was always adamant about the point that this was her own choice to believe and follow the Bahá'í teachings. To be clear, the prison interrogator would almost certainly not have been one of the guards in the arrest. This conflation of character is for dramatic purposes.

81. "*He took many days, but since then, he's been quite useful to us.*" (II, i, 54)

    Mr. Mahmúdnizhád and other arrested members of the Shiraz Spiritual Assembly were initially each given 74 lashes and were sent into solitary confinement. According to Mrs. Mahmúdnizhád, "the prisoner was made to lie down on his stomach and his hands and feet were tied to the bed. Then using a three-layered cable, or a gas hose, or a whip, the prisoner was lashed. There was a man by the name of Abdu'llah who was called to do the whipping. He was supposed to put the Qur'an under his arm and whip the prisoner with the sort of force that would still enable him to keep the Qur'an under his arm; however, he was cruel and never used the book. He raised the whip as far as he could, and lashed the prisoner with all his might. The men were whipped on their naked bodies and were left on the bed with blood streaming down their flesh, so that they would be whipped again on the next day on their injured bodies. This was done to pain the prisoners to a state that would move them to recant their faith." She then lists the women who were tortured thus. She also comments on the severity of torture faced by her husband.

Mona was confronted with her father in the described condition. They told him they would torture her unless she start to answer their questions. Mrs. Mahmúdnizhád describes the encounter: "He asked the authorities to allow him to speak to his daughter… and father and daughter were blindfolded and brought face to face. He told his daughter: 'please convey the truth as you know it. We have no underground secrets or anything of that sort. If we have rendered any service to the community, we have only fulfilled our religious obligation.' … They took father and daughter back to their cells. After some time, they went to Mona's father again and told him that they would whip Mona if he could not convince her [to talk.] Mona's father then asked them to open their blindfolds so that they could see one another... Mona had also asked that their blindfolds be removed. She had told them that the eyes were windows to the heart and that if she were able to see her father's eyes, perhaps she could be moved to accept her father's request. In this way, father and daughter were able to see each other in prison once again. It was a beautiful meeting. They hugged and kissed, and Mona accepted her father's request. These two dear souls met twice; once they were blindfolded and once they were not." Mrs. Mahmúdnizhád then describes the third and final meeting they had, which is dramatized in Act II, Scene 6.

Now up until that point, the Bahá'í prisoners had held a united front of silent resistance. When Mr. Mahmúdnizhád—in his condition—started counseling the Bahá'ís to tell the truth, questions and doubts arose. He was so well-respected, but was he right or even trustworthy some wondered? Eventually, everyone started to go along with this new strategy of openness.

82. "*So your world center in Israel isn't political!*" (II, i, 55)

A common accusation from the Iranian government and clergy is that the Bahá'ís are spies for Israel or America. This absurd contention is backed up by saying the Bahá'í World Center is in Israel. As Mr. Mahmúdnizhád argues here, the World Center is in Israel because Bahá'u'lláh, the Prophet-Founder of the Bahá'í Faith, was banished from His homeland of Iran by the Persian and Ottoman governments to Iraq, then Turkey, finally being locked up in the prison city of Akka, Palestine. This all happened a good eighty years before the establishment of Israel.

Accusations of spying are nothing new. More than a century ago, the Baha'is were accused of spying for Britain or Russia, when those countries were seen as Iran's great political rivals. This clearly represents a pattern of scapegoating with no basis in fact.

83. "*You want me to get 'Abdu'llah?*" (II, i, 55)

    See Note 81.

84. "*Ya Baha'u-l'abha!!... Let me see his eyes...*" (II, i, 56)

    It is believed that Mona's father was tortured in front of Mona to get her to talk. Mona's mother spoke delicately about the idea: "Mona did not like to speak about the emotional tortures that she suffered inside the prison, especially things that would cause me to worry. However, it is possible that this [witnessing her father being tortured] may have happened a few nights after she was arrested."

85. "*In a vision,* MONA *sees the* WOMAN IN WHITE *at the door, radiant, watching the* FATHER *wheeled off. Then, the door opposite opens and fire seems to pour in.*" (II, i, 57)

    This vision is fictional, but it is another attempt to glimpse Mona's subjective experience when she did have her visions.

86. "*Let me get the Magistrate.*" (II, i, 57)

    As part of the Islamic Revolution, a new judicial system was set up that advanced the laws of the new theocratic state. The *Religious Magistrate* would then be a judge within these *Revolutionary Courts.* Áyatu'llah Qazá'í was the powerful religious cleric who sentenced Mona and the other 9 women to be executed. After some time, he was himself accused of some crime, arrested and tortured, losing an eye in the process.

87. "*Sweetheart, we're going to let you go. Don't worry, we just need you to do a little paperwork.*" (II, i, 58)

    Once the Bahá'í prisoners began to open up, they faced a mountain of paperwork. They would need to fill out forms by hand while sitting on the cement floor for hours. The questions Mona said she was asked in her first interrogation, according to The Story of Mona, were:

"What is your religion? What do you believe in? Were you born in a Bahá'í family? Date and place of birth. Name of the school you are studying at. Which grade? Have you ever taught in a Bahá'í class? When did you declare and who was present at that session? Names of the members of the Local Spiritual Assembly of Shiraz and the members of the Bahá'í National Spiritual Assembly. What activities do you do as a Bahá'í? Names of the members of the Bahá'í committees in Shiraz. Write about the Bahá'í administration. How many members of the Universal House of Justice are Persian and how many are not? What nationalities are they? Names of all the prominent international Bahá'í administrators in the world. Have you ever been on pilgrimage? How much have you donated to the Fund? Who was the chairperson of the feast and where was it held? Who did you vote for this year? Have your parents been members of the Local Spiritual Assembly? The name of the Bahá'ís you know. Are you willing to recant?"

The authorities probably did expect to let Mona go. It's important to keep this in mind in performing the piece, as well, and not to make her execution a foregone conclusion. Mona's father was in a different category. He would be considered an apostate, because he had personally converted from Islam to the Bahá'í Faith, and death is the punishment for apostasy.

88. "TARANEH *carries a baby girl, little* NURA. *The* MOTHER *has Mona's release paper in her hand.*" (II, ii, 59)

As mentioned above (Note 31), Taráneh had given birth to Nura in January 1982.

After the arrests, the Bahá'í prisoners' families were not allowed to visit for many weeks, though they came in crowds together with the families of political prisoners and waited outside the jail. Announcements of executions of the latter group would fill the families with anguish and the rest with pity. After four weeks, the head of the police station created a diversion for the Revolutionary Guard to allow the Bahá'í families to see their loved ones. Even then, they were only able to stare at each other silently through glass for a few minutes. Taráneh burst into tears and Mona gestured for her to wipe away her tears.

This scene combines a few different days' events, the first of which was when the possibility of Mona's release had come up. Mona told her mother during one visit that the prosecutor had told her she could be freed if they paid 200,000 Tuman (about $50,000-$75,000 US). Her mother rushed away to request help from the Spiritual Assembly. The answer came back that it was unwise to give in to this request as it would set a precedent for extortion and that the bail amounts would no doubt rise astronomically. The mother gently told Mona the news and Mona accepted the news with almost joyful detachment.

89. "*Is it possible to come in? I'd like to freshen up before my visit, you understand.*" (II, ii, 59)

Mrs. Mahmúdnizhád and others used to go to the prison several times a week not expecting a visit but just to see if there was any news. On these long waits, there were not adequate facilities for them. Mrs. Mahmúdnizhád also had kidney problems. One such day was 20 January, 1983 when she was approached by an Interrogator who asked her if she were Mona's mother. He said he had some questions for her. She knew that if she didn't give the same answers that Mona did, Mona would be lashed. She refused to answer, saying she was not his prisoner. He had a guard watch her, walked out, and returned with an arrest warrant, saying that now she was his prisoner. She was then put through an extensive interrogation with no access to a rest room or a glass of water, both of which she needed greatly with her kidney trouble.

90. "*O God, I want my child. I want Mona from you. I want to touch her, to kiss her cheek…*" (II, ii, 60)

After those initial four weeks of not being able to see Mona, her mother broke down and just started begging God. This version of her prayer is taken from Olya's Story, p. 134. It was the following day that she was given that first silent visit (described in Note 88).

91. "*What more do you need from me? You have my husband, you have my daughter. Maybe I have a few questions for you.*" (II, ii, 61)

During this 20 January interrogation that went on for many hours, Mrs. Mahmúdnizhád got sicker, more fatigued and nauseated. The interrogator didn't stop though. Some of her responses were quite pointed, and he idly threatened her with whipping. At the end, he gave her the option to go to Sepah jail or to go to Adelabad prison. She said "I wish to go home." Since it was the weekend and there was no one to take her to the prison, he agreed, but said she needed to present herself in just over 24 hours or pay 500,000 Tuman. She did present herself that Saturday morning and would spend 5 months in prison thereafter.

92. "ARAM *picks up the torn release form.*" (II, ii, 61)

    The business with the release form, torn and taped back together in the following scene, is all fictional.

93. "*I just overheard something: he's going to start executing women.*" (II, iii, 62)

    In 1983, the Revolutionary court in Shiraz changed tactics and began executing women. To tie by implication this decision to one cleric's anger at Mrs. Mahmudmizhad is fictional, but it makes dramatic sense given the narrow scope of the play.

94. "*It's just a piece of paper.*" (II, iii, 62)

    Shí'ih Islam has a teaching called *taqiya*, which allows Muslims to dissemble their Faith if they are being persecuted. They often assume Bahá'ís should have the same thing. Regarding this, Bahá'u'lláh wrote, "In this Day, We can neither approve the conduct of the fearful that seeketh to dissemble his faith, nor sanction the behavior of the avowed believer that clamorously asserteth his allegiance to this Cause. Both should observe the dictates of wisdom, and strive diligently to serve the best interests of the Faith." (Bahá'u'lláh, Gleanings from the Writings of Bahá'u'lláh, p. 343)

95. "*If they kill us, Aram, God will raise up others greater than us.*" (II, iii, 62)

    The spiritual principle that sacrifice now ultimately reaps greater rewards in the end is a universal one. Compare Mona's line to Bahá'u'lláh's words recalling His own darkest moments in the Siyah-Chal prison: "One night, in a dream, these exalted words were heard on every side: 'Verily, We shall render Thee victorious by Thyself and by Thy Pen. Grieve Thou not for that which hath befallen Thee, neither be Thou afraid, for Thou art in safety. Erelong will God raise up the treasures of the earth—men who will aid Thee through Thyself and through Thy Name, wherewith God hath revived the hearts of such as have recognized Him.' " (Bahá'u'lláh, Epistle to the Son of the Wolf, p. 21)

96. "*Doesn't it make sense that I am here in front of you, apparently chosen by God, to remind you…?*" (II, iii, 63)

    This interaction is fictional.

97. "*I don't have enough gas to get home, my mother has our cash.*" (II, iv, 64)

This moment is fictional, but it joins together a couple of true incidents. While her mother was detained and interrogated for all those hours, Taráneh had no idea what was going on or what to do. Her baby was sick with pneumonia, barely able to breathe. Still Taráneh waited. Mrs. Mahmúdnizhád, after arguing that the interrogator should let her go home, realized she had no money, no ride and it was after midnight. She walked back to the interrogator's office and asked him to lend her 5 Tuman for a taxi, which he did!! When she walked out though, Taráneh was still there with her head resting on the steering wheel, baby sleeping in the back seat. That tiny softness of heart of the interrogator in giving her money was a beautiful element I felt like I had to include. She returned the 5 tuman when she turned herself in.

98. "*It's night.* MONA *and several other women are blindfolded in a staggered line.*" (II, v, 65)

Mock executions were used frequently to terrorize and to ferret out the psychologically weak who would then go for further interrogation. Olya Roohizadegan describes undergoing this as she was lined up with other women prisoners. She also comments on how fear was replaced by a sense of freedom and release, until they realized it was just a ploy. This particular scene is fictional, and the appearance of the Woman in White is meant to embody that lightness and freedom. It might be a stretch to have a mulla with a machine gun, but here he's acting more like a prison warden, again representing authority for the sake of dramatic economy. Incidentally, blindfolded prisoners would be led about by grabbing the end of a rolled up newspaper held by the guard, thus avoiding direct contact since Bahá'ís are considered "unclean."

99. "*It was like a world of love and light opening up to us. I don't know why we're still here.*" (II, vi, 67)

At a certain point, the hardship and meaninglessness of imprisonment leads some to prefer death, since it would be a release. Add to that the beautiful expectations of the next world held by the Bahá'ís, it is even more understandable. We can infer that Mona went into prison hoping to get out, but at a certain point, there was a transition, which is fictionally represented in the following scene (Scene 7).

100. *"Mom?... What are you doing here?"* (II, vi, 67)

After spending three months on the outside worried about her two loved ones in prison, Mona's mother was now in herself. She describes riding to Adelabad prison in a bus full of Bahá'í prisoners, women in the front separated from men in the back. All had just received death sentences, and they all started laughing uproariously at this, as if they were all going to a feast or wedding. She continues: "When we reached the ward, they [the female Bahá'í prisoners] all hugged me, kissed me, and welcomed me… The last one to greet me was Mona. She put her arm around me and said, 'come mother; I want to show you your new home.' She took me to a cell, which housed one bed…" She and Mona shared the cell with Mrs. Tahirih Siyavushi, who was martyred with Mona.

101. *"The* FATHER *and* TARANEH *are separated by a glass barrier and they speak through phones."* (II, vi, 67)

This was the standard visitation allowed between immediate family members and the prisoners, where ideally they might have 10-20 minutes of time to talk over a phone through glass.

102. *"I feel left out, like God has forgotten me. Wasn't I worth being imprisoned for my Faith too?"* (II, vi, 68)

Taráneh was torn up about being the only one still out of prison. She struggled with sadness, emptiness and questions of her own value. The language here is quite close to what Taráneh and her father said in what would be their final visitation in early March 1983. His words brought her into the circle of suffering, and he told her with sincerity to be happy and be confident. (The Story of Mona)

103. *"It's important to keep the right attitude in here—"* (II, vi, 68)

One can recognize in the record two dominant strains in the Mother's emotions upon arriving in prison: bewilderment and deep disgust at prison life and hygiene, and an almost smothering joy at being with Mona again. She was not accustomed to the hardship of prison, and her health concerns and overall sensitivity provoked a lot of anxiety in her. Mona and many others were learning to make the best of the situation in there. Mona had thrown herself into serving others, including the prostitutes, drug addicts and political prisoners who shared their ward. Mona would help the addicts through withdrawal, saving some of her own food for them. She would help clean them, draw pictures for them, sing songs, tell them stories and encourage them in their lives. Everyone loved Mona despite the fact that the prison authorities had forbidden the Muslims interacting with the Bahá'ís.

104. "*Last night, a husband and wife, recanted the Bahá'í heresy. Now they are free!*" (II, vi, 68)

Mrs. Mahmúdnizhád describes a large meeting where the authorities were trying to convince the Bahá'ís to recant. One individual from a Bahá'í family—she says he was actually a communist—was paraded about in this meeting as having recanted his faith. The prosecutor signed his release there in front of everyone, and the families were allowed a visitation in hopes that they would discuss this.

Olya Roohizadegan was released just before Mrs. Mahmúdnizhád arrived, and she describes in her book a Bahá'í couple that did recant in that period. The wife was put through unusually rough interrogations and enormous psychological pressure involving her young children. In her final trial, she recanted her faith. The husband later recanted, in order to protect his wife who was being hounded by guards since her Bahá'í marriage was now void. This story was used for propaganda purposes by the prison authorities and the government-run press.

105. "*My wife, from Bahá'u'lláh, our inheritance is prison. From the Báb, martyrdom.*" (II, vi, 69)

This scene captures briefly a number of the elements of the family's final meeting, including this call to heroism in response to her despair at what would become of her when he was gone. Mrs. Mahmúdnizhád said, "Mr. Mahmúdnizhád looked at me with compassion and said to me, 'do you remember that every time we wanted to move to a new home, I would go clean the house, send you to a friend's home, move our furniture into the house, and then I would shower, wear my best clothes and take you to our new home with a new decor. I want to do the same for you now. I will go to the Realm on High and make the necessary preparations, I will then come to take you there.' These words created a great feeling in me, and today I am still surviving on his promise and am counting the days for the appointed day to arrive."

106. "*Are you heavenly or earthly?*" (II, vi, 69)

Mona hadn't seen her father in four months. According to her mother, they didn't speak, but communicated through their eyes. Mona kept rising up and kissing his eyes, while he spoke to the Mother. He asked Mona this one question. Mona replied, and he stood up, snapped his fingers and said "Let's go!"

107. "*Yadu'lláh Mahmúdnizhád. Rahmatu'lláh Vafáí. Túbá Zá'irpúr.*" (II, vi, 70)

On 12 March, 1983, Mr. Mahmúdnizhád was hanged along with two other Bahá'ís, including Mrs. Za'irpur, who had been together with Mona since the night of her arrest and who had been mercilessly tortured.

108. "*May my life be sacrificed for you.*" (II, vi, 70)

This is actually a common expression in Persian, "fadát besham," often used when one is moved emotionally or sometimes as a sign of gratitude in polite conversation. Here obviously the meaning reaches deeper than just the platitude.

109. "*Won't you congratulate me, friends? My father has been martyred for his faith, and I am so immensely proud of him.*" (II, vi, 70)

There were fears and rumors that Mr. Mahmúdnizhád had been executed, but Mona and her mother didn't hear officially until a visit with Taráneh a week later. Mona returned to the cell block, spoke words of pride in her father, and then went to pray alone. From that time on, according to one source, Mona's disposition changed. Mrs Mahmúdnizhád said, "I frequently saw Mona crying and asking to be executed so that she could be in the presence of Bahá'u'lláh and her father. She was crying and asking that her blue cape be changed to the red cape."

110. "*It's been a full day: she doesn't eat, she doesn't talk.*" (II, vii, 71)

One day in early June, Mona entered an intensive period of fasting and praying. According to her mother, "She did not eat or drink for about 30 hours after she had that dream and spent all night in prayer and meditation. Finally, she began to eat after 30 hours and said, 'Mother, I was delivered!' I never asked her what she meant by having been delivered!" About a week or so later, Mona had a vision or dream one night where 'Abdu'l-Bahá came to her and asked her three times what she wanted, to which she replied each time "perseverance." His response was "It is granted. It is granted." (This is dramatized at the end of this scene on p. 75.)

111. *"Where are you tonight, Mona? I can't find your star."* (II, vii, 71)

As mentioned earlier (Note 65), this story was shared by Mona's friend, Tahmíneh. She shared the following with Mrs. Mahmúdnizhád, "As God is my witness, at the beginning of each month, I start looking at the sky at night, in search of the brilliant star. On the evening that it finally appears, I gaze at it for hours and shed tears and burn with the fire that blazes in my heart with my love for Mona. My husband and children also love to look at that star. Yes, that brilliant star is my radiant Mona who comes to us and then again hides herself from us."

112. *"The prison though has shifted. There's no one around, no sound, and there are hints in the lighting that eternity waits behind these walls."* (II, vii, 72)

Up until now, the play has mostly remained on the plane of the physical with several glimmerings of the spiritual world. This scene shift is a projection into that spiritual world. Obviously, there is no clear account of Mona's experience during her meditation period. We know she emerged detached and luminous. Given the thematic vocabulary of the play to this point, I have tried to enact a reversal in the character Mona's perspective by rousing her awareness and showing her the point of view from the spiritual world. As is said, "the rules are different here" and "here you are strong." Justice and injustice from that point of view are conceptions limited to the earthly plane.

113. *"This is the world of light."* (II, vii, 72)

This is a synonym for the spiritual world or heaven in Bahá'í understanding and language. This physical world, by contrast, is seen as a world of both light and darkness.

114. *"I would like to trade my blue and black dresses for the red."* (II, vii, 73)

See Note 109.

115. *"God can work through me too, right, Mona? You're so... beyond where I am. If you don't see any hope for me..."* (II, vii, 74)

This is the essential insight of the play, where the character Mona learns to see past the narrow boundaries of names and the sharp judgment of the moment, to perceive in any and every human being the image of God and the ever-present possibility of change and hope.

116. "*What is it that you want? Perseverance.*" (II, vii, 75)

See Note 110.

117. "*How radiant you are.*" (II, vii, 75)

Early one morning, in what would be their final week in prison, Mrs. Mahmúdnizhád was suffering greatly with kidney pain and with emotional agony. Her daughter had been trying to tell her the night before that she foresaw her own martyrdom. She went so far as to describe what would happen as if it were a play. Not having slept, the mother went for a walk around the cell block. Returning to the cell, she saw Mona seated in prayer looking "absolutely divine." Overcome with emotion, she ran to interrupt her and share her feelings. This is when Mona shared her vision of a world transformed, of youth arising, and of her willingness to give a thousand lives.

118. "*Maybe a family is not what I want or need.... What I really want is bigger than that. I want to see this world changed, Mom.*" (II, vii, 76)

The monologue here is based on Mona's words to her mother, sharing her vision of world unity and her willingness to make the greatest sacrifices to bring it about. After hearing her daughter's vision, Mrs. Mahmúdnizhád was transformed: "It was then that I submitted completely to the Will of God, in such a manner that I wished the authorities would come right at that moment and take us all to the arena of our martyrdom."

119. "*The* MOTHER *goes to the chair but doesn't sit down; instead she stands with her hand on the chair and pretends to be deaf.*" (II, viii, 77)

The details and dialogue of the Mother's trial here are all taken from her account, even the comedic bits such as pretending to be deaf and the typing of 'hello'. Her trial though was actually in January before she was sent to Adelabad prison. [See Notes 89 & 91.]

120. "*Your parents have deceived and misled you.*" (II, viii, 78)

These lines and most of what follows thereafter are paraphrases or quotes from Mona's final trial, which was with Ayatu'lláh Qazá'í. In this trial, he also brought up the tapes of her chanting, saying "You are accused of misleading youth with your beautiful voice and chanting. Now I am sure about the charges against you." (The Story of Mona)

121. "*Now if by Islam you mean the hatred and bloodshed going on in this country, now that is the reason I'm a Bahá'í!*" (II, viii, 78)

This line is a paraphrase of something Mona said to the Religious Magistrate and is recorded in several accounts. The fearlessness it took to make this statement to one of the most powerful clerics in the city is hard to appreciate. All the other prisoners marveled at the 'little prisoner' when news of this spread. Mona's fearlessness was well-understood by the interrogators and guards as well.

122. "*We must obey the Qur'an. Accept Islam or face execution / I kiss the order of execution.*" (II, viii, 78)

Excerpted from Olya's Story, p. 133.

123. "*Mrs. Mahmúdnizhád, you wanted to know what your sentence was?*" (II, viii, 79)

This punishment to spend her life in mourning for her husband and daughter was actually pronounced by the judge in her trial. (Though, when asked to clarify, he said 'death.') The former sentence though was to be her fate. She was released from prison only five days before Mona was executed. The family was allowed one more visit with Mona, apparently the day of the execution. It was a poignant and emotional meeting.

Despite her frailty, Mrs. Mahmúdnizhád was a heroine in her own right. Imprisoned for her faith, she ended up suffering gravely. She dedicated much of her life to telling the story of her famous daughter and saintly husband.

124. "*Take her, put her with the other nine. Hang them one at a time from oldest to youngest. This one will be the last.*" (II, viii, 80)

Ten women were sent to the gallows that night of 18 June 1983, only two days after six men had been similarly executed. The women were taken by bus to an abandoned polo field. They went singing and chanting, with poise and confidence. They were hanged one-by-one starting with the oldest and leaving Mona to the last.

125. "*I'll tell them what you've done here.*" (II, ix, 81)

The bus driver was so moved by what he had seen that night, he came and told the Bahá'ís the story. This is how we know some of what happened. Word of Mona kissing the hand and then the rope came out. I don't know of any documentation of this, but she had said to her mother when she was describing her coming execution that she would first kiss the hand of her executioner, and then kiss the rope with which she was to be hanged.

126. "*'Izzat Ishráqí. Nusrat Yaldá'í. Táhirih Síyávushí. Zarrín…*" (II, ix, 81)

These are the names of Mona's fellow martyrs, in descending order of age:

'Izzat Ishráqí

Nusrat Yaldá'í

Táhirih Síyávushí

Zarrín Muqímí

Mahshíd Nírúmand

Shírín Dálvand

Símín Sábirí

Akhtar Sábet

Royá Ishráqí

Mona Mahmúdnizhád

Each of them has a story, and each of them deserves a play of their own. After the execution, their bodies were taken to a morgue to be identified by their families, and then they were dumped without ceremony in a mass grave in the Bahá'í cemetery. The play doesn't, however, end on the earthly plane with its sadness and its injustice. It follows the martyrs into the world of light. It is in glimpsing that vision that we allow their stories to aid in our own transformation.

Persian Pronunciation Guide (Simplified)

Observing just a few rules, a Persian accent can be fairly well approximated from a transliterated word or name. *

1. Vowel sounds

   a. When vowels have accents

      á sounds like "a" in "father" or "o" in "dog"

      í sounds like "ee" in "cheese"

      ú sounds like "oo" in "shoot"

   b. When vowels have no accents

      a sounds like "a" in "cat"

      e or i sounds like "e" in "get"

      o or u sounds like "o" in "go"

2. Consonant sounds

   a. Most consonant sounds are similar to English.

   b. Kh, Gh, and Q are guttural sounds, unfamiliar to English speakers. Appropriately, "kh" is midway between a "k" and an "h" and "gh" (and "q") is midway between a "g" and an "h." These are difficult sounds for many, so an easy compromise is pronouncing "kh" as "k," and "gh" (and "q") as "g."

   c. The "zh" sound is like the French "j" or the "s" in "treasure." This sound is in the name "Mahmúdnizhád."

3. Stress

   a. In general, give all syllables more or less equal stress.

   b. Fight the English tendency to speak in iambs or any other stressed / unstressed combination.

* For pronouncing character names, see the character list at the beginning of the play for proper transliteration. For Persian and Arabic terms with proper accents, see the Glossary.

Notes on Readings

Readings are good low-budget ways to experience plays. If you would like to do a reading (that is, have a group read the play out loud), there are a couple of things to consider:

First, you will want to decide if you want a formal or informal reading. In a formal reading, the room is divided between readers and audience, the way a theatre generally is. In the stage area, there is a chair for each reader. (In this play, you may want 7 or 8 readers all together: 1 for stage directions, the rest for characters.) Each reader has a script, while the audience generally does not. In other ways, the formal reading follows the basic rules of theatre-going. Some preparation or rehearsal is important. For most occasions, one or two group "read-throughs" before the presentation will be sufficient. Taken further, "staged readings" incorporate some blocking (or stage movement), more developed scene work, and even simple props. In a less formal reading, such as one might want in a classroom or study circle, everyone will probably have access to a script, and, depending on the size of the group, the character roles can either be spread out more or heaped up higher.

Second, this play takes place in Iran, and the readers should be prepared for the Persian and Arabic words they will encounter. (See *Persian Pronunciation Guide*, p. 129) A single foreign word can cause a hiccup in a reading, but a string of them can induce cardiac arrest. "Mahmúdnizhád," for example, is a mouthful and is said many times throughout the play.

Bibliography

'Abdu'l-Bahá, Paris Talks. London: UK Bahá'í Publishing Trust, 1972.

'Abdu'l-Bahá, Promulgation of Universal Peace. (Comp. by Howard MacNutt). Wilmette, IL: Bahá'í Publishing Trust, 1982.

'Abdu'l-Bahá, Selections from the Writings of 'Abdu'l-Bahá. (Trans. by Marzieh Gail and committee). Wilmette, IL: Bahá'í Publishing Trust, 1997.

'Abdu'l-Bahá, Some Answered Questions. (Trans. by Laura Clifford-Barney). Wilmette, IL: Bahá'í Publishing Trust, 1930.

A Dress for Mona (website). Ed. Mark Perry. Rev. Jan 2008. Drama Circle. http://www.adressformona.org

Anonymous, "Mona's Life." (Trans. by Azadeh and Mark Perry) Drama Circle. http://www.adressformona.org

Bahá'í National Youth Committee, Unrestrained as the Wind. Wilmette, IL: Bahá'í Publishing Trust, 1985.

Bahá'u'lláh, Epistle to the Son of the Wolf. (Trans. by Shoghi Effendi). Wilmette, IL: Bahá'í Publishing Trust, 1941.

Bahá'u'lláh, Gleanings from the Writings of Bahá'u'lláh. (Trans. by Shoghi Effendi). Wilmette, IL: Bahá'í Publishing Trust, 1952.

Bahá'u'lláh, The Kitáb-i-Aqdas (The Most Holy Book). Haifa: Bahá'í World Centre, 1992.

Bahá'u'lláh, The Kitáb-i-Íqán (The Book of Certitude). (Trans. by Shoghi Effendi). Wilmette, IL: Bahá'í Publishing Trust, 1931.

Bahá'u'lláh, The Seven Valleys and the Four Valleys. (Trans. by Marzieh Gail). Wilmette, IL: Bahá'í Publishing Trust, 1952.

Bahá'u'lláh, Tablets of Bahá'u'lláh, revealed after the Kitab-i-Aqdas. (Trans. by Habib Taherzadeh and committee). Wilmette, IL: Bahá'í Publishing Trust, 1988.

Bahá'u'lláh (et al), Bahá'í Prayers. Wilmette, IL: Bahá'í Publishing Trust, 1954.

Mahmúdnizhád, Farkhundih, "Notes for a Film." (Trans. by Gloria Shahzadeh). Unpublished account of correspondence with Jack Lenz and Alexei Berteig, 2001.

National Spiritual Assembly of the Bahá'ís of Canada, The Story of Mona: 1965-1983. Thornhill: Bahá'í Canada Publications, 1985.

Perry, Mark, A Dress for Mona. Shoreham, VT: 5th Epoch Press, 2002.

Roohizadegan, Olya, Olya's Story. Oxford: Oneworld Publications, 1993.

The Bahá'í World, Vol. XIX: 1983-1986. Prepared under the supervision of The Universal House of Justice. Haifa: Bahá'í World Centre, 1994.

Drama Circle (website). Ed. Mark Perry. Rev. Mar 2008. Drama Circle. <http://www.dramacircle.org>

Zarandi, Nabíl ('Azam), The Dawn-Breakers: Nabil's Narrative of the Early Days of the Bahá'í Revelation. (Trans. and ed. by Shoghi Effendi). Wilmette, IL: Bahá'í Publishing Trust, 1932.

Mark Perry teaches playwriting and play analysis at the University of North Carolina at Chapel Hill and serves as a dramaturg for Playmakers Repertory Company. He is a graduate of the University of Iowa's Playwrights Workshop. His other plays include *On the Rooftop with Bill Sears*, *Band of Gold* and *The Will of Bernard Boynton.*